SUGAR DADDIES

by Alan Ayckbourn

samuelfrench.co.uk

FOR AMATEUR PRODUCTION ENQUIRIES

UNITED KINGDOM AND WORLD
EXCLUDING NORTH AMERICA

plays@samuelfrench.co.uk

020 7255 4302/01

Each title is subject to availability from Samuel French,
depending upon country of performance.

Acting Editions

BORN TO PERFORM

Playscripts designed from the ground up to work the way you do in rehearsal, performance and study

---

Larger, clearer text for easier reading

Wider margins for notes

Performance features such as character and props lists, sound and lighting cues, and more

---

+ CHOOSE A SIZE AND STYLE TO SUIT YOU

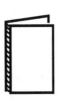

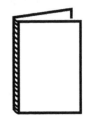

STANDARD EDITION

Our regular paperback book at our regular size

SPIRAL-BOUND EDITION

The same size as the Standard Edition, but with a sturdy, easy-to-fold, easy-to-hold spiral-bound spine

LARGE EDITION

A4 size and spiral bound, with larger text and a blank page for notes opposite every page of text – perfect for technical and directing use

LEARN MORE | **samuelfrench.co.uk/actingeditions**

**Other plays by ALAN AYCKBOURN
published by Samuel French**

This Is Where We Came In

Time and Time Again

Time of My Life

Tons of Money (revised)

Way Upstream

Wildest Dreams

Wolf at the Door

Woman in Mind

A Word from Our Sponsor

**Other plays by ALAN AYCKBOURN
licensed by Samuel French**

The Boy Who Fell Into a Book

Invisible Friends

The Jollies

Orvin – Champion of Champions

Surprises

Whenever

**FIND PERFECT PLAYS TO PERFORM AT
www.samuelfrench.co.uk/perform**

ABOUT THE AUTHOR

Alan Ayckbourn has worked in theatre as a playwright and director for over fifty years, rarely if ever tempted by television or film, which perhaps explains why he continues to be so prolific. To date he has written more than eighty plays, many one act plays and a large amount of work for the younger audience. His work has been translated into over thirty-five languages, is performed on stage and television throughout the world and has won countless awards.

Major successes include: *Relatively Speaking, How the Other Half Loves, Absurd Person Singular, Bedroom Farce, A Chorus of Disapproval,* and *The Norman Conquests.* In recent years, there have been revivals of *Season's Greetings* and *A Small Family Business* at the National Theatre; in the West End *Absent Friends, A Chorus of Disapproval, Relatively Speaking* and *How the Other Half Loves*; and at Chichester Festival Theatre, major revivals of *Way Upstream* in 2015, and *The Norman Conquests* in 2017.

Artistic Director of the Stephen Joseph theatre from 1972–2009, where almost all his plays have been first staged, he continues to direct his latest new work there. He has been inducted into American Theater's Hall of Fame, received the 2010 Critics' Circle Award for Services to the Arts and became the first British playwright to receive both Olivier and Tony Special Lifetime Achievement Awards. He was knighted in 1997 for services to the theatre.

Image credit: Andrew Higgins.

AUTHOR'S NOTE

The climax to *Sugar Daddies* was altered in 2013, prior to
the US premiere at ACT (A Contemporary Theatre), Seattle.
Therefore the script presented here is different from any
previously published versions. Speaking at the time about the
reason for the changes, Alan Ayckbourn said the following:

"Rereading the play, I thought Sasha goes through this
experience pretty well unscathed. She escapes with just a singe.
I wanted those last few moments to show that there's part of
Uncle Val that's been left with her. If you've supped with the
devil, you've probably burnt your tongue. There is a sense
that Sasha is refreshingly clear-eyed at the beginning, the
'country mouse' who has come into the city, but she has a sort
of mistrust of human nature by the end - something you see in
children growing up.... Sasha's not quite the girl she was at the
beginning; she has developed a ruthlessness."

*(from an interview with Thomas May for Crosscut.com,
3 October 2013)*

MUSIC USE NOTE

Licensees are solely responsible for obtaining formal written permission from copyright owners to use copyrighted music in the performance of this play and are strongly cautioned to do so. If no such permission is obtained by the licensee, then the licensee must use only original music that the licensee owns and controls. Licensees are solely responsible and liable for all music clearances and shall indemnify the copyright owners of the play(s) and their licensing agent, Samuel French, against any costs, expenses, losses and liabilities arising from the use of music by licensees. Please contact the appropriate music licensing authority in your territory for the rights to any incidental music.

IMPORTANT BILLING AND CREDIT REQUIREMENTS

If you have obtained performance rights to this title, please refer to your licensing agreement for important billing and credit requirements.

FIRST PERFORMANCE INFO

World Premiere at Stephen Joseph Theatre, Scarborough:
Round auditorium on 22 July, 2003.

With the following cast:

Sasha	ALISON PARGETER
Val	REX GARNER
Chloe	ANNA BRECON
Ashley	TERENCE BOOTH
Charmaine	ELIZA HUNT

Director: ALAN AYCKBOURN
Design: ROGER GLOSSOP
Lighting: MICK HUGHES
Costumes: CHRISTINE WALL
Music: DAVID NEWTON

The North American Premiere took place at ACT, Seattle
(Allen Theatre) on 10 October 2013.

With the following cast:

Sasha	EMILY CHISHOLM
Val	SEÁN G. GRIFFIN
Chloe	ELINOR GUNN
Ashley	JOHN PATRICK LOWRIE
Charmaine	ANNE ALLGOOD

Director: ALAN AYCKBOURN
Design: MATTHEW SMUCKER
Sound: BRENDAN PATRICK HOGAN
Costumes: DEB TROUT
Lighting: RICK PAULSEN

CHARACTERS

SASHA – early 20s
CHLOË – her half sister, early 30s
VAL – late 70s
ASHLEY – late 70s
CHARMAINE – mid 60s

SETTING

The living room of Chloë and Sasha's London flat.

TIME

ACT I
Scene One: 6pm. A few days before Christmas.
Scene Two: 6pm. Two weeks later.
Scene Three: 2am. That same night.
Scene Four: 6pm. Two days later.

ACT II
Scene One: Mid-day. Several weeks later.
Scene Two: 7pm. A few days later.
Scene Three: A few hours later. The same night.
Scene Four: The next morning.

ACT I

Scene One

The living/dining, all-purpose room in CHLOË's *and* SASHA's *first floor London flat. Although the flat is a large, pleasant, airy Victorian conversion, the furnishings and décor are rather run down, due to lack of care rather than money. At the start, it is an untidy shambles, with abundant evidence of the two women who live there. Clothes and belongings, especially* CHLOË's, *are strewn everywhere. Amidst the debris, there are some signs that it is just before Christmas, with one or two cards and a tiny, rather battered artificial tree.*

*Furnishings include a sofa, an armchair with accompanying coffee table, a rarely used extendible dining table with three chairs and a desk (*CHLOË's*) strewn with papers. These virtually bury the phone and her laptop. Also a sideboard with drawers and cupboards. There are three doors leading from the room. The flat's front door which opens directly onto the first floor landing. Besides this is an entry phone linked to the downstairs street door. A second door leads to the kitchen; a third to the flat's two bedrooms, etc.*

It is late December, just before six pm and outside it is dark. At the start, the room is lit only from the street lights outside. We can hear the continuous rumble of city traffic.

In a moment, there is the sound of voices outside the flat's front door. They are those of SASHA *and* VAL. *His*

*is pure cockney whilst hers has the slight trace of a
Norfolk burr.*

SASHA *(offstage)* ...just these last few stairs. Are you sure you
can manage alright?

VAL *(offstage)* ...I can do it, my dear, you mustn't worry about
me...

The sound of a key in the lock.

SASHA *(offstage)* Here we are. Here at last.

VAL *(offstage)* ...so kind of you, my dear. As I say, you're a good
Samaritan...

*The front door opens and light from the landing
illuminates the room. At first silhouetted, we catch our
first glimpse of* SASHA *and* VAL.

SASHA *is in her early 20s. Her casual clothing and rather
well scrubbed face, with no trace of make up, tend to
make her appear younger. Her manner is direct and
open. All in all she appears friendly, straightforward
and unsophisticated. She is assisting* VAL *who is in
his late seventies or even early eighties. He is limping
slightly having recently injured his leg. We can see little
of the rest of him initially as he is dressed in a Father
Christmas outfit complete with beard.* SASHA *switches
on the lights. The full horror of the room is revealed.*

SASHA There!

VAL *(a little startled by his surroundings)* My word!

SASHA Sorry, it's a bit... We've been meaning to...but neither
of us seems to get round to it. *(Clearing the armchair of
clothing)* Here. Why don't you sit here, while I get you the
water?

VAL Thank you, my dear. *(Indicating the dining chairs)* Would
it be alright if I sat in one of those...?

SASHA *(hastily making a dining chair accessible)* Oh, yes of course.

VAL Only if I sat down in that one, I doubt I'd be able to get up again.

SASHA Right.

VAL I tend to lock up. I could be here for the duration. *(He sits)*

SASHA That OK?

VAL Ideal. This is ideal. Couldn't be bettered.

SASHA *(moving to the kitchen)* I'll fetch the water.

SASHA goes off briefly to the kitchen.

VAL *(calling after her)* You're a good Samaritan, my dear. I say, a veritable good Samaritan.

VAL surveys the room briefly.

(to himself) Dear, oh dear, oh dear!

VAL fumbles under his robe and retrieves a sachet of tablets from his pocket. SASHA returns with a glass of water.

SASHA Here you are.

She hands it to VAL who hesitates.

It is clean, I promise. I rinsed it. In running water.

VAL I'm sure you did. *(Extracting the pills from the foil)* You're very kind.

SASHA *(solicitously)* Can you manage those?

VAL I can manage. Take a couple of these, I'll be right as rain. Just for the old ticker, you know...

SASHA Yes.

VAL For the shock. *(Taking the glass from her)* Ta.

SASHA *(indicating his beard)* Do you need to take off your – beard, first? I mean, does it come off?

VAL Oh, yes, it comes off. *(He has his hands full)* I don't wear this all year.

SASHA Here. Let me. *(She helps to remove his beard)*

VAL Ta. You're a good, kind girl. *(Indicating pills)* These'll put me right. I just take two of these. Just for the shock. I'm not supposed to give it too many shocks. If I do that I get told off by my doctor...

SASHA Well, it wasn't your fault just now, was it? It was their fault entirely. I was a witness. The only witness. You weren't even on the road. You were walking on the pavement, weren't you – are you alright?

VAL *(who seems to have a little trouble swallowing)* Fine. Right as rain, now.

SASHA I could crumble them up for you, if that would make them easier to swallow.

VAL No, you've done enough, you've done quite enough, dear.

SASHA I'm used to doing that. I used to do it for my Auntie Fay. Before she died.

VAL Well, I'm not dead yet. Not long to go, probably, but not dead yet.

SASHA No thanks to that driver. Didn't even stop, did they? Just to drive off and leave you lying there like that.

VAL Sign of the times, my dear...

SASHA I mean, you could have been dead. You could have been dead for all they knew...

VAL ...times we live in. It's called urban disregard...

SASHA ...or at least, badly hurt. How's your leg now?

VAL I think it's just a bruise, dear. Nothing more.

SASHA Are you sure?

VAL Just my hip. I've been very lucky.

SASHA I still think you should get it looked at.

VAL No, no. No need for that.

SASHA You can never be sure. Especially when you get to – to certain stages in life, you know...

VAL Don't you worry. I'm a tough old git. Always have been. Car didn't touch me, you see. I jumped out of the way and banged into the wall, that's all. Saw him just in time.

SASHA What was it doing driving on the pavement?

VAL It's that time of year, darling. Every other driver's over the limit, isn't he? Full of Christmas spirit, no doubt. Take your life in your hands, going out walking this time of the year.

SASHA Where were you going, anyway?

VAL I just come out the hospital, didn't I?

SASHA (alarmed) You'd been in hospital, as well?

VAL No, no. Not that way. I was visiting. Children's hospital. On the corner of Melbourne Street. Just along there. Doing my good deed for the year.

SASHA Oh, I see. Father Christmas.

VAL Been doing it sixteen years.

SASHA Lovely.

VAL Bring the presents. Little walk round the beds. Have a word with the kiddies. Cheer 'em up. Have a little joke. I always keep the kit on when I leave though. 'Cause some of them, the ones that can walk like, they look out the windows. Otherwise it would spoil it. Park the car round the corner.

SASHA I bet they must love it.

VAL I don't know about them. I certainly do. Wouldn't miss it. See the little faces. Innocence, you know. At that age, they really believe in you. Father Christmas. Still young enough to believe, you see.

SASHA Yes. I can remember that.

VAL You used to believe, did you?

SASHA *(a trifle embarrassed)* Yes, I believed. I believed right till I was eleven.

VAL Goodness! That'd be your mum and dad did that then?

SASHA Right. They used to go to all sorts of lengths. We got this big log fireplace at home, and they used to fetch soot down the chimney. On Christmas Eve. As if he'd actually climbed down, you know. And they'd leave sooty footprints right across the living room floor to the kitchen.

VAL What, all over your carpet?

SASHA No, it's stone. We have a stone floor.

VAL Oh, I see.

SASHA Right through to the kitchen. And then on the table, on the kitchen table, they'd have left him a glass of milk and some mince pies.

VAL Right.

SASHA Covered up, you know. Last thing at night. And in the morning, they'd be all gone. Just crumbs and the empty glass. Like he'd been there.

VAL Gracious.

SASHA And there'd be like handprints everywhere. Sooty ones, you know. Where he'd touched things.

VAL Quite a mess.

SASHA It was. They had to have the place re-painted every other year.

VAL They sound like loving sort of people.

SASHA *(smiling)* They are.

VAL I take it you're an only?

SASHA Yes.

VAL Ah. That'd do it.

SASHA They both run this tea room. My dad cooks and my mum runs it.

VAL Where's this then?

SASHA In Swaithe.

VAL Swaithe? Where's that?

SASHA Not far from King's Lynn.

VAL looks blank.

In Norfolk.

VAL Norfolk. That's where you're from?

SASHA Right.

VAL Yes. I thought I – you know, spotted a – an accent.

SASHA Did you? Have I still got one? I thought I must have lost it by now.

VAL How long you been in London?

SASHA Oh, coming up two months.

VAL Well, you still got one. Norfolk. Just north of me, then.

SASHA You live up that way?

VAL Essex.

SASHA *(doubtfully)* Ah.

Slight pause.

VAL Listen my dear, I won't take up any more of your time. I'd best be moving along. You've been a real good Samaritan...

SASHA But how are you going to get home? To Essex?

VAL Look, what I'll do is, you don't have to worry, I'll make a quick call, if I may, to my nephew Frankie. And ask him to come and pick me up.

SASHA You sure?

VAL He won't be a minute. He'll be somewhere in the neighbourhood, he's bound to be. He was supposed to pick me up in the first place only he must have missed me.

SASHA *(moving to the desk)* There's a phone over here somewhere – if I can find it...

VAL Don't bother, no bother. I got my own one here. *(He fishes for his mobile)* Present from my grandchildren. They give it me for just such an emergency.

SASHA You have a lot of grandchildren?

VAL *(as he dials)* Fifteen. At the last count. Ranging from thirty-two, Adam, right down to six, little Melanie-Ann. Adam's from my eldest son Bernie's second marriage to Lainey, and Melanie's from my youngest daughter June and her first husband Wayne. Only they just split up. Excuse me, one minute, dear.

SASHA Of course.

During **VAL**'s *phone call,* **SASHA** *goes back to the kitchen briefly with the water.* **VAL** *walks about during the next.*

VAL *(into his mobile)* Frankie? Where'd you get to, you pillock? ...I was waiting on the corner of Melbourne, wasn't I? ...Frankie, I said half five...half <u>five</u>... Well, you're no bloody use to me in a betting shop, are you, son?

SASHA *returns and hovers in the doorway.*

(aware of her, moderating his tone slightly) Yes, you come and pick me up now, there's a good lad, Frankie... Yes, I'm at – *(To* **SASHA***)* Where am I exactly, darling, can you tell me?

SASHA 56 Widcombe Street.

VAL 56 Widcombe Street... You got that? Well, it's just round the corner from Melbourne Street, isn't it? ...No, that's Birdsmoore Street. Widcombe Street... Yes, well you just get your – yourself round here Frankie... I'm with a very nice, kind young lady whose name I don't even know, who has kindly come to my rescue.

SASHA Sasha.

VAL Sasha. That's nice... *(Into phone)* No, I'll tell you later. Blow by blow. Just get here pronto, son.

SASHA First floor. Tell him to ring the bell marked Vines. Flat two.

VAL Oy, Frankie. Ring the bell marked Vines... Vines. First floor... No, <u>first</u>. See you in a minute, son. *(He rings off)* Nice boy with all the intellect of a fridge magnet. That's a pretty name that – Sasha.

SASHA Thank you. Do you want to sit down again, till your nephew arrives?

VAL No, sweet of you, but I can't sit down for too long, see, else they'll lock up completely. The knees.

SASHA Your knees?

VAL Like that. *(Demonstrating with his hands)* They stiffen. Solid.

SASHA Do you know what's wrong with them?

VAL Over-age and over-usage. That's the medical term. Past their stroll-by date. My work, that was. Lot of kneeling involved.

SASHA *(mystified)* Kneeling? In your work?

VAL That or crouching.

SASHA What were you then? A vicar?

VAL Vicar? No, policeman.

SASHA Oh.

VAL Thirty four years.

SASHA Here in London?

VAL Serious crime squad, mostly. Chief Super.

SASHA Right.

VAL Retired. Wasn't much I didn't see, I can tell you.

SASHA I bet.

VAL All changed now.

SASHA Yes?

VAL For the worst. No honour, you see. Used to be honour. No honour these days.

SASHA No?

VAL Everyone for himself.

SASHA You think so?

VAL End of civilisation, my dear. Just around the corner.

SASHA I hope not. I'm just starting out.

VAL *(smiling)* Don't you worry. You'll be fine. Sasha. Sasha. Your parents choose that for you, did they?

SASHA Yes.

VAL I'm Val, by the way.

SASHA How do you do?

VAL Everyone calls me Uncle Val. Always has done.

SASHA Right.

VAL You can call me Uncle Val if you like.

SASHA *(smiling)* OK.

He smiles at her.

VAL Nice big flat. You live here on your own do you, Sasha?

SASHA Oh, no. I share it with my sister. Chloë.

VAL I thought you said you was an only?

SASHA Oh, yes. Sorry. My half sister. Chloë's my half sister. Only her mother died. Quite young. And her father then married my mother. Only Chloë doesn't speak to our father any more. So we never met. Not till recently.

VAL I see.

SASHA Chloë's older than me.

VAL She owns the flat, does she?

SASHA No, we both do. Well, neither of us does. We rent it. Together. She had someone else sharing with her. Only they left – they didn't get on – and I was just about to come here to college and – so it worked out quite conveniently, in the end. I don't know how much longer we'll be able to afford to live here, though.

VAL Why's that?

SASHA Well, they're apparently putting the rents up by a fantastic amount – like double – they've just written to tell us. It is pretty cheap at the moment, I suppose. For London, anyway. They're probably justified. So I think we may have to move. I mean, Chloë's earning pretty well – she works in television, she's a researcher – but I'm just a student, of course. And I don't think she can afford the place on her own. And there's very few people she'd choose to share with. 'Cos she doesn't get on, not with everyone, you see.

VAL Who's your landlord, then?

SASHA No idea. Some company or other. Perry – Perry something. I did know. Periphon. Periphon Properties.

VAL Periphon?

SASHA Have you heard of them?

VAL No.

SASHA The people downstairs. The Pearsons. I think they've already decided to move out. *(Realising she's been rabbiting on rather)* Anyway. *(Slight pause)* She should be home soon. Then I have to go out again.

VAL On the town, eh?

SASHA What? Oh, no. To work.

VAL I thought you were a student?

SASHA I am. This is just a night job.

VAL Doing what?

SASHA Washing up, mostly. Working in a hotel kitchen. The Dorchester.

VAL Nothing but the best, then.

SASHA I wouldn't know. Dirty plates are dirty plates, aren't they? I haven't a clue what was on them originally.

VAL And what's it you're studying, Sasha?

SASHA I'm at catering college. North London.

VAL Ah, I see. You want to run a tea room like your mum and dad, do you?

SASHA Not really, no. I want to run my own restaurant. Eventually.

VAL What, in Norfolk?

SASHA London. Essex. Not fussed.

VAL I'll tell you what, you come to Essex. We could do with a few more good eating places out our way.

SASHA *(smiling)* I'll bear that in mind. Or I might be a singer. I can sing quite well. Only I don't like singing in public. Not at present.

VAL That's a drawback, then.

SASHA Not till I've practised a bit more. But then I might end up singing in my own restaurant. When I'm not cooking. I'll have to see. Who knows?

VAL Leave it open for now, eh?

SASHA Yes.

VAL Plenty of time, isn't there? Tell me, did you by any chance get a sight of the driver? In that car?

SASHA What, the one that nearly...? No. It was all so quick. I couldn't even swear it was a him. Drove away so fast.

VAL Right. So you didn't happen to notice if they had one eye?

SASHA One eye? What makes you think they had one eye?

VAL Well, it would explain the driving. I mean, I understand that with only one eye, it's more difficult to judge distances. So that could explain it.

SASHA *(puzzled)* No, I didn't notice.

VAL Just a long shot.

Pause.

SASHA He shouldn't even have been driving with one eye, anyway, should he?

VAL *(darkly)* That never stops most of them.

The sound of a key in the front door lock.

SASHA Oh. This'll be her. My sister.

CHLOË *enters. In her early thirties, she is somewhat fraught. This is more or less the norm for her. She is trying to keep up with the pace of modern living and under all manner of pressure both at work and in her personal life. Almost the complete reverse of her younger half sister.*

CHLOË *(as she enters)*...that is the last bloody time I am travelling on that Northern Line, I can tell you that. Why the hell can't people find another way to kill themselves? Why must they always choose <u>my</u> train to plunge themselves in front of –? *(Seeing VAL, stifling a scream)* Oh my God, who are you?

SASHA It's OK, Chloë, it's OK.

CHLOË Who is he? What's he doing here?

VAL How do you do? I'm –

CHLOË Sasha, who is he?

SASHA He's –

CHLOË How did he get in here?

SASHA I let him in.

CHLOË You let him in? Why d'you let him in?

SASHA Val was – he was nearly run down in the road. I brought him back here so he could recover.

CHLOË *(incredulous)* You brought a stranger back to this flat?

SASHA Yes, as I say –

CHLOË A man you've never even met before? A complete stranger off the street and you bring him back here –? My God, Sasha, what's the matter with you, girl? Are you completely and utterly half-witted? He could be anyone, couldn't he? Anyone? Look at him! What do you know about him, do you even know the first thing about him?

SASHA Chloë, he was hurt in an –

VAL How do you do, I'm –

CHLOË Who is he? Tell me, who the hell is he?

SASHA *(loudly)* Chloë, he's perfectly alright, he's Father Christmas!

Silence.

CHLOË *(softly)* He's what?

SASHA And before that he used to be a policeman.

CHLOË A policeman?

SASHA He's called Uncle Val.

CHLOË You mean he's a relative?

SASHA No –

CHLOË He's certainly no relative of mine, I can tell you that.

VAL Listen, I do beg your pardon. I didn't mean to startle you. I'm just on the point of leaving. Your sister's been very kind and helpful...

CHLOË'*s mobile rings.*

CHLOË God! I've only just come in the door! *(She answers it)*

VAL ...and I won't impose on you any further.

CHLOË *(into phone)* Hallo...

VAL I'll wait out in the street, Sasha. Frankie'll be along in a minute.

CHLOË *(into phone)* Hallo... I can't hear you, you're breaking up!

SASHA No, you can wait here. You don't have to –

VAL Be best, I think. *(To* CHLOË*)* I'll be off then. Good-bye.

CHLOË *(ignoring* VAL, *into phone)* Hallo! Oh, Mr Bagwick, it's so – Ragwick, sorry – It's good of you to call back so late... No. Let me tell you what this is. My name's Chloë Vines, I'm a researcher with – no, Vines – V – I – N – E – S ...Yes...

As she speaks, CHLOË *struggles out of her coat which she tosses casually onto a chair. She seats herself at the desk, still talking.*

SASHA *(during this, sotto to* VAL*)* I'm sorry. I think my sister's had a rough day.

VAL That's quite alright. I've outstayed my welcome.

SASHA Not at all!

CHLOË *(under this, into phone)* ...no, I do see... It would be literally five minutes...no, absolutely...we would respect your privacy utterly... I don't know if you know the programme at all, but we never...no, we never...we wouldn't... No, we absolutely wouldn't, not under any circumstances...listen, maybe you'd care to sleep on it? May I call you in the morning? Mmm... Mmmm... Mmmm... Mmm...

SASHA *lets* VAL *out of the front door.*

VAL Good-bye then, Sasha.

SASHA Good-bye then – Uncle Val. (*Just before closing the door)* Go carefully now, won't you? Look both ways...

CHLOË *(into the phone)* ...right, just as you like, Mr Wagwick. Either way you have our complete assurances that we'll absolutely respect your decision...of course...of course...

VAL *leaves.* SASHA *finally shuts the door.*

...yes, lovely to talk to you, too... Bye. *(She rings off)* God, that man's a pain in the arse...all we want is a five second sound bite... *(Looking round, to* SASHA*)* Have you got rid of him?

SASHA Yes, he's gone now.

CHLOË God, Sasha! What did you think you were doing? How many more times? You are not in Great Yarmouth now, girl.

SASHA King's Lynn.

CHLOË We are in the middle of London where nowhere, repeat nowhere, these days is safe and I've told you, you let no one into your home unless it's burning to the ground and you're absolutely convinced it's the fire brigade. As for bringing strange men in without a by your leave –

SASHA He was very nice.

CHLOË Oh, yes? How could you possibly know that? How could you possibly?

SASHA I could tell. He used to be a policeman.

CHLOË A policeman! Anyone can say that. Don't do it again. Don't ever let strangers in here again. Ever.

SASHA Sorry.

CHLOË Not that we're going to be here much longer. The Pearsons downstairs, they're definitely going. She told me this morning. They're going to stay with her brother-in-law temporarily. End of next week they're off. *(In pain)* Aaaah! God, I need a bath. *(Hunching her shoulders)* Aaaah!

SASHA Bad day, again?

CHLOË It's my shoulders. Aaah! Aaah! Aaah! Tension! I've had the most ghastly day. Just awful. Would you believe, I spent hours working on this item and then at the very last minute, Marjorie decides to cut it. I mean, why let me spend hours on something if she meant to cut it?

SASHA Perhaps she didn't know she wanted to cut it.

CHLOË How do you mean?

SASHA Until the last minute.

CHLOË Oh, she knew, she knew alright. Don't tell me she didn't know.

SASHA *(giving up)* Well.

CHLOË *(rolling her head)* Aaaah! I'd been working on it for three solid days. And nights. I wouldn't mind but it isn't the first time she's done it. You didn't let that man in the bedrooms, did you?

SASHA No. He just sat on the chair there.

CHLOË Only sometimes they – you know – they do things in the drawers.

SASHA Really? I don't think he's like that.

CHLOË You don't know. You've no idea. You're just a child, Sasha. Welcome to inner city hell, darling. The sooner you get back to – Leighton Buzzard – the better for you.

SASHA *(softly)* King's Lynn. Everyone here seems very friendly to me.

CHLOË Ha! Ha! Ha!

SASHA I'd better get changed for work, I suppose. You're out tonight, aren't you?

CHLOË *(grimly)* No.

SASHA Oh. I thought you were.

CHLOË I thought I was, too. Until I get this text message at 4 o'clock this afternoon.

SASHA Oh. From Zack, was it?

CHLOË Who do you think? Hasn't even got the guts to speak to me to my face. Just a bloody text message. I mean – a text message. Want to see?

SASHA Not really.

CHLOË No, go on. See for yourself. You won't believe this. *(She punches her phone buttons)* Look. How would you feel if someone did this to you?

SASHA I don't have a phone.

CHLOË Look at this. What sort of person would write this to someone?

SASHA *(reading with difficulty)* "Thnk we shd cl it..." What's cl?

CHLOË Cool. I think.

SASHA ...cl it. Nd to fnd my spce...

CHLOË Need to find my space, that is. What space? I couldn't give him more space if I tried.

SASHA Tk sn. Z. X.

CHLOË Bloody men. Well, that's it. This time. No more. He has had it. Goodbye, Zack.

SASHA You have said that before, you know.

CHLOË This time I really mean it. No, I really, really mean it, Sasha. I do. Really.

SASHA Yes.

CHLOË You don't believe me but I do.

SASHA I just think he's – playing you around a bit, that's all. It's all about when it suits him, isn't it? You don't come into it.

CHLOË *(defensively)* Well, I do. It's – it's an open relationship. Two way. I mean, it's when it suits me too. As well. You know.

SASHA It never seems to be.

CHLOË How do you mean?

SASHA When it suits you. It always seems to be when it suits him, doesn't it? That's how it seems to me.

CHLOË *(considering this)* You're too young to understand. When you get to my age... Anyway, let's not talk about it, it's over. Over! The next time Zack tries to get in touch, I'm not available, do you hear?

SASHA *(unconvinced)* Good.

CHLOË I mean it, Sasha.

SASHA I must get going.

CHLOË Sod him! I'll have a wonderful evening on my own. Wash my hair. Wallow in a hot bath. Watch garbage TV. Have an early night. Hot water bottle. Pamper myself.

SASHA Why not?

CHLOË Have we got any of that gin left?

SASHA I think you drunk it all.

CHLOË Did I? I don't remember that. When did I drink it?

SASHA Last week. When Zack phoned to say he wasn't –

CHLOË Oh, yes. You need the bathroom first?

SASHA No, you go ahead.

CHLOË I mean, how can anyone just text you? It's unimaginable. I can't believe someone could do that to another human being, can you?

CHLOË's mobile rings again. She grabs at it, glances briefly at the display and answers it.

(as she goes) Roger, darling, how can I help? Yep...yep...yep...

CHLOË *goes off to the bedrooms.*

SASHA *(to herself, surveying the room)* I really must have a good tidy up sometime. You can't see to think in here.

She turns to follow CHLOË *when the front door buzzer rings.* CHLOË *returns with her blouse half unbuttoned, still talking.*

CHLOË No...no...no... *(To* SASHA*)* Who's that?

SASHA *(going to the entry phone)* No idea.

CHLOË Not that old man back again, I hope? *(Into her phone)* Yep...yep...

SASHA *(picking up the entry phone)* Hallo? ...Who? ...Oh. Right. Hang on. I'll be down. *(She hangs up)* It's some flowers, apparently.

CHLOË *(touched)* Ah! *(Into phone)* Roger, could you hang on just one second, darling? *(To* SASHA*)* Could you get them, I'm...?

SASHA Sure. *(As she goes)* I suppose this means it's all on again now, does it?

SASHA *goes out.*

CHLOË *(after her)* No it does not, not at all. *(Into phone)* Roger, may I call you back, darling? ...Yep, OK... Sure will. Bye.

CHLOË *rings off. During the next, she takes off her blouse and tosses it casually on to a chair.*

(calling through the doorway to SASHA*)* It'll take more than a measly bunch of flowers to get round me this time, I can tell you. He's tried it all before. It's not going to work. Not this time. My mind is absolutely made up. Nothing in this world is going to – oh!

SASHA *returns with a huge bunch of expensive looking flowers.* CHLOË *gawps.*

SASHA What about these then?

CHLOË God, they're gorgeous! Must have cost him a fortune.

SASHA *(presenting* CHLOË *with the flowers)* Who still loves you, then?

CHLOË Well... Nonetheless. It'll still take more than a bunch of flowers. He needn't think he's going to buy his way back with these, I can tell you.

She puts them down and starts to open the card.

He must think I was born yesterday. He wants to see me again, it'll take more than this. I tell you, he'll have to come crawling through that doorway on his hands and –

She breaks off and stares at the card.

(dead) These aren't for me.

SASHA They're not?

CHLOË They're for you. I think they must be for you. *(She hands* SASHA *the card)*

SASHA *(reading)* "To my little Samaritan. With love and thanks. Uncle Val." *(She smiles)* That's nice.

CHLOË *(stamping out)* God! I just don't believe it! Bloody men!

CHLOË *goes off again to the bedroom with a scream.*
SASHA *picks up the flowers and smells them.*

SASHA *(smiling again)* They're lovely...

As she stands there:

A blackout.

End of Scene One

Scene Two

The same.

Two weeks later. Six pm.

The room is (comparatively) tidier. Someone, presumably
SASHA, *has made some effort.* CHLOË *is busy laying
the table. She is going to a good deal of trouble. It is
clearly intended to be a romantic candlelit dinner for
two. During the next,* CHLOË *bustles about laying the
table whilst simultaneously talking on her mobile.*

CHLOË *(as she works)* ...no...no...well, I told her that... I told
her that... David, I told her that...at the meeting...yes... I
told her that...because she never listens to me, David...well,
I don't know what to say... Are you telling me we have to
do it all over again? Because she can't make up her bloody
mind? ...Well, that's what you seem to be saying, David...

The front door opens and SASHA *comes in. She is dressed
in her casual college clothes and coat. She carries, amidst
all her other clobber, a smart dress shop carrier bag. She
waves to* CHLOË *who vaguely acknowledges her.*

...well, that's what it sounds like to me, David. You can wrap
it up in...no, you can wrap it up...you can wrap it up in...

SASHA *puts down her bags and goes into the kitchen
briefly.*

David, the fact is, I don't feel wanted any longer. I don't feel
needed, I don't feel necessary. Everything I do is wrong or
inadequate... It is, David. It is... Well, if that really is the
case...then I'd like to hear I was valued, occasionally... I'd
just like a little acknowledgement. A little appreciation...

SASHA *reappears from the kitchen. She is swigging from
a bottle of water.*

Listen, David, I can't discuss this now. I'm expecting people for dinner, I have to go... Yes, alright...yes... Alright. Bye. *(She rings off. To herself)* He doesn't give a stuff.

CHLOË *seems as if she might be about to cry.*

SASHA Hallo.

CHLOË *(muted)* Hi.

SASHA *takes off her coat.*

The atmosphere seems a bit cooler between them.

Cutting it a bit fine, aren't you? I thought you were going out?

SASHA I am.

CHLOË What time's he supposed to pick you up?

SASHA Half six.

CHLOË Then you'd better get a move on, hadn't you? I'm expecting Zack here soon after seven. If I don't get another text message in the meantime.

SASHA I'll be gone by then, don't worry. *(Returning to the kitchen)* The traffic was really terrible...

SASHA *goes off briefly.*

CHLOË *(calling after her)* Could you bring that bottle of wine off the table?

SASHA *(offstage)* Right.

CHLOË *(calling)* Traffic? Didn't you come home by tube?

SASHA *(offstage)* No.

CHLOË *(calling)* You didn't risk the bus, surely?

SASHA *returns with an opened bottle of claret.*

SASHA *(evasively)* No, I –

CHLOË *(incredulous)* A taxi?

SASHA *(reluctantly)* No, actually, Frankie picked me up in the car...

CHLOË *(blankly)* Frankie?

SASHA Uncle Val's nephew Frankie.

CHLOË In the car?

SASHA Yes.

CHLOË All the way from Hendon?

SASHA Right. Felt a bit grand. Coming out of a hygiene class and straight into a Roller.

CHLOË *(coolly)* Well, it's alright for some, isn't it?

SASHA Bit of a laugh. They all cheered.

CHLOË I just hope you know what you're doing, Sasha, that's all.

SASHA I'll be alright. Looks good. In there. What you're cooking. Looks good.

CHLOË I'd hardly call it cooking. Re-cycling I think is the word. Still, we can't all be cordon bleu cooks, can we? Even if we could spare the time.

SASHA *(gathering up her things)* I must get changed.

CHLOË *(seeing the dress bag)* What have you got there?

SASHA Just a dress.

CHLOË New?

SASHA We're going out. I had nothing to wear.

SASHA *goes off to the bedroom.*

CHLOË Since when could you afford to shop in Bond Street, for God's sake? *(To herself)* I just pray she knows what she's doing. *(Calling)* Oh. Incidentally, one piece of very good news, Sasha. The management agent phoned me today. They're not going to increase the rent, after all.

SASHA *(offstage)* They're not?

CHLOË *(calling)* Would you believe? They've obviously had a change of heart. Which is virtually unheard of from them.

SASHA *(offstage)* What happened?

CHLOË *(calling)* The woman didn't give a reason. I don't think she even knew. Just passing on the message. That's a huge relief, isn't it? I think the poor old Pearsons must be kicking themselves. Moved out too soon, didn't they? Oh, and I think the new people have already moved in downstairs. I caught a glimpse of someone when I came in earlier. The man, anyway. I presume it's them. He looked a bit sinister. I hope they're alright. I'm really going to miss the Pearsons. They were always so useful, whenever I wasn't here to –

The front door buzzer rings.

God, that can't be Zack already, surely? *(Going to the entry phone and answering)* Hallo...? Oh, yes. Right. Push the door. *(She hangs up)* *(Calling)* Sasha, it's your... Val man.

SASHA *(offstage)* Oh, right. Tell him I won't be a minute.

CHLOË *(calling)* Well don't leave me alone with him for too long, will you?

CHLOË *fusses with the table arrangement some more. The flat doorbell rings.*

(calling) Just a minute.

CHLOË *opens the front door and admits* VAL. *He is in evening dress, looking very smart, in contrast to his first appearance. He carries a small bunch of flowers.*

(startled) Oh.

VAL Good evening.

CHLOË Come in.

VAL Thank you, Chloë. Call you Chloë, can I?

CHLOË Yes, of course. Val.

VAL *steps in to the room.*

CHLOË *closes the door.*

Sasha's just – finishing getting ready.

VAL I'm a trifle early.

Pause.

Can't rush a woman, can you?

CHLOË *(smiling frostily)* No.

Slight pause.

Would you care to sit down?

VAL No, I'd rather not, if you don't mind.

CHLOË Just as you like.

VAL I – tend to stiffen up.

CHLOË Do you?

VAL The knees.

CHLOË Ah.

VAL Besides, we'll be sitting all evening.

CHLOË Where are you going? Is it a pop concert?

VAL The Royal Opera House.

CHLOË Oh.

VAL *(indicating his bouquet)* Bought her a little bunch.

CHLOË How sweet.

VAL I know she likes flowers.

CHLOË Yes. Well, we all – like flowers – most of us.

Pause.

I'd offer you a glass of wine – Val – only – that's all I have, I'm afraid. And I'm expecting someone – shortly.

VAL That's quite alright, my dear. I drink very sparingly these days.

CHLOË Do you?

VAL Ever since... *(He taps his chest)*

CHLOË Oh, I see.

VAL Finish me off completely.

CHLOË *(with a rather forced laugh)* Well, we can't have that, can we?

They both laugh.

SASHA *enters. She is now wearing her new dress and looks terrific. The effect is demure and not too revealing. She glows.*

SASHA Hallo, sorry.

VAL Well, look at that. Would you just look at that, Chloë. A vision of loveliness, Sasha. You look absolutely stunning, my dear.

SASHA *(a little self-consciously)* Thank you. These shoes alright with it you think, Chloë?

CHLOË *(rather tight-lipped)* Lovely.

VAL Perfect. *(Presenting* **SASHA** *with the flowers)* These are for you.

SASHA Oh. That's really nice. *(To* **CHLOË***)* He knows I'm fond of flowers.

CHLOË *(smiling brightly)* Yes.

SASHA *(moving to the kitchen)* I'll just put them in water.

SASHA *goes off briefly.*

CHLOË It is. A lovely dress. I don't know how she can afford dresses like that.

VAL Ah, well. Therein lies a secret.

CHLOË Yes?

VAL There was a little arrangement we came to –

CHLOË You mean you bought it for her?

VAL Oh, no, no, no. Nothing like that. I would never do that. Ours is not that sort of relationship.

CHLOË What sort of relationship is it, exactly?

VAL It's a gradually growing friendship.

CHLOË Really? *(She laughs)* Well, we all know those, don't we?

VAL If you don't mind me saying so, Chloë, I think you have a rather jaded view of mankind.

CHLOË No, just men.

VAL Ah, well. No doubt justified through bitter experience?

CHLOË No doubt.

VAL Returning to the dress, I have a friend who runs a little boutique and I called in a favour from her, that's all.

CHLOË I see.

SASHA returns from the kitchen.

VAL I was just explaining to Chloë, Sasha, our little deal with the dress shop.

SASHA His little deal, you mean. I don't know how he does it. Anything I wanted for ten quid, she said. Unbelievable. Are you sure, I said? Oh yes, she said. I owe Uncle Val one. Help yourself. Val knows people everywhere. Flower shops, car parks, boutiques... National Gallery...

VAL Well, Sasha, when you've lived as long as I have, you make a few friends. A few contacts. You're bound to. Ready for off, are we?

SASHA I've only got my ordinary coat, I'm afraid, will that be alright? I managed to find this bag, second hand, but I couldn't find a coat that would go. Not in the time.

VAL That'll be fine, we're only going as far as the car. Here, allow me.

VAL puts the coat around SASHA's shoulders.

SASHA Thank you.

VAL Nephew Frankie awaits. Have to see if we can't find you a coat as well, won't we? I may have a contact or two.

SASHA We'll see about that, Uncle Val. You can't keep on spoiling me, can you now? *(To CHLOË)* See you later, Chloë.

VAL *(opening the door for SASHA)* Good-bye, Chloë. *(Confidentially)* She may be a trifle late. We're going on after.

CHLOË *(stunned)* Right.

SASHA *(as they go)* You know, I've never ever been to the opera.

VAL There's always a first time.

SASHA What is it we're seeing, then?

VAL First night of *The Flying Dutchman.*

SASHA *The Flying Dutchman?*

VAL By Richard Wagner. You familiar with Wagner?

SASHA I've heard of him.

The door closes behind them. CHLOË stands in a slight state of shock for a moment.

CHLOË *(softly)* My God!

She pulls herself together and turns her attention back to the table. She glances at her watch, then back at the table.

(to herself) Matches...

She moves to the kitchen.

(as she goes, incredulously) The Flying Dutchman?

CHLOË *goes off. A silence for a second or two. Then, on the table, her mobile bleeps, announcing an incoming text message. Silence.* CHLOË *returns with the matches. The mobile bleeps again. There is evidently a page two of the message.*

(in quiet despair) Oh dear God, no. *(Hurrying to the phone)* No, no, no!

As CHLOË *picks up her phone and prepares to read her message, the lights fade to: –.*

Blackout.

End of Scene Two

Scene Three

The same.

The room is lit only dimly by the street lights through the curtains.

It is now around 2am the same night. CHLOË *is flat out on the sofa, a crumpled mess. The wine bottle, now empty, lies on the floor beside her. So does an empty half bottle of gin.*

She appears to have used the same glass. Apart from that, the table is unchanged, still laid up for the meal that never happened, the candles unlit.

In a moment, the sound of a key softly in the front door lock. SASHA *enters, the hall light behind her, still in her opera gear and with her coat round her shoulders. She is a little drunk. She creeps in and closes the door but doesn't switch on the light, anxious not to disturb* CHLOË, *whatever she might be up to. Consequently, as she crosses the room using the furniture as guides towards finding the bedroom, she puts her hand unwittingly on* CHLOË*'s upturned face.*

SASHA *(squawking)* Aaah!

She gropes around, discovering the rest of CHLOË.

(alarmed) Chloë? Chloë? Chloë?

SASHA *makes her way with difficulty back to the front door. She switches on the room lights.*

(seeing CHLOË *clearly for the first time)* Oh, God!

SASHA *hurries back and tries shaking* CHLOË *awake, but she is like a limp rag doll. She might even be dead.*

Certainly SASHA *thinks she might be. She hurries back and opens the front door.*

(yelling down the stairs) Val! Uncle Val! Frankie!

She hurries back to CHLOË *again, leaving the front door open.*

Chloë! Chloë! Talk to me, Chloë! Please!

She runs to the windows this time and sticks her head out.

(yelling into the night) Help! Help! Somebody help me!

She returns to CHLOË *once again.*

Please, Chloë! Please, say something. Please, don't be dead! You mustn't be dead!

She runs back to the front door. As she reaches it, ASHLEY *appears in the doorway. He is in his seventies, also a Londoner and a slightly sinister figure. He is wearing a dark silk dressing gown and slippers. He has a black patch over one eye.* SASHA *all but runs into him. She jumps back.*

(another involuntary squeak) Ah!

ASHLEY *(darkly)* Do you mind telling me what the hell is going on up here?

SASHA *(breathless)* It's my – it's my – my sister. She's there – she's – I don't know if she's dead. She could be dead. Please, could you help me, please?

ASHLEY *(suspiciously)* What makes you think she's dead?

SASHA She's just lying there. She's not moving. Just lying.

ASHLEY It's the middle of the night, isn't it? People often just lie there in the middle of the night. That's what they're supposed to do at two o'clock in the morning. That's what's intended. It's called sleeping. Maybe you're unfamiliar with that? You lie there, quietly, until it gets light. And that allows other people to go to sleep as well. Especially people like me, who happen to be unfortunate enough to live downstairs, underneath you. Now keep it down, alright?

SASHA I'm sorry. *(She swallows, then hiccups)*

ASHLEY Have you been drinking?

SASHA Yes.

ASHLEY Are you drunk?

SASHA Yes. I've been to see *The Flying Dutchman.*

ASHLEY Have you now?

SASHA Yes.

ASHLEY Well, I hope he's managing to get some kip.

SASHA Could you please look at my sister, please?

ASHLEY *(suspiciously)* Why should I want to look at your sister?

SASHA To see if she's alive. Please.

> **ASHLEY** *enters the room and goes over to* **CHLOË.** *He examines her with a certain expertise.* **SASHA** *watches him, holding her breath.* **ASHLEY** *straightens up.*

Well?

ASHLEY She is what is medically known as pissed as a newt.

SASHA Drunk?

ASHLEY Even worse than you are.

SASHA Are you sure?

ASHLEY I'm surprised you can't smell her. She's practically fermenting here. *(Picking up the empty wine bottle)* This may have something to do with it. *(Picking up the gin bottle)* Or failing that, this certainly will have.

SASHA *(taking the bottles)* Oh.

ASHLEY Happy? Alright if I go back to bed now, is it?

SASHA I'm sorry.

ASHLEY starts to move away.

Er –

ASHLEY What?

SASHA You couldn't possibly help me with her?

ASHLEY Eh?

SASHA Just as far as the bedroom? Please?

ASHLEY *(grudgingly)* Alright.

SASHA Thanks.

ASHLEY I'm not undressing her.

SASHA No.

ASHLEY I'm not getting into any of that.

SASHA No, that's fine, I'll do that bit.

ASHLEY appraises the task for a second.

ASHLEY Right. I'll lift her, you take the other side. Ready?

SASHA Ready.

ASHLEY Hup!

SASHA Hup!

They both struggle with the limp CHLOË *who comes round slightly.*

CHLOË *(drowsily)* Mmm...mmmuuuurrr...mmm...mmmmuuuu rrr... *(Seeing* ASHLEY*)* Oh, dear God. Who are you?

SASHA *(soothingly)* It's alright, Chloë. This kind gentleman is helping me.

CHLOË *(alarmed)* Another one?

SASHA He's just a friend.

CHLOË How many more of them have you got?

SASHA *(to* ASHLEY*)* I think she's a bit delirious. *(As they move off, conversationally)* You've just moved here, you say?

ASHLEY This afternoon. Downstairs...

SASHA *(struggling)* Right...

ASHLEY And if there's any more of this, I'm moving out.

They all go off. In a moment, SASHA *and* ASHLEY *return.*

SASHA *(a little breathless)* Thank you so much. You're very kind.

ASHLEY *is breathing slightly wheezily.*

Are you alright?

ASHLEY I get – chest trouble... I'll be alright.

SASHA Can I get you something? A drink?

ASHLEY I could accept a glass of water.

SASHA Sure.

ASHLEY Bottled.

SASHA Of course.

SASHA *goes off. As soon as she is gone,* ASHLEY *prowls the room, studying it carefully. He picks up papers and opens drawers.* SASHA *returns with a glass of water.*

Here you are.

ASHLEY *(taking the glass)* Ta. *(He sips the water)*

SASHA Would you care to sit down?

ASHLEY Just for a minute, then.

SASHA Unless you stiffen up.

ASHLEY Unless I what?

SASHA I have this friend. About the same age as you. If he sits down he tends to stiffen up.

ASHLEY Does he? Lucky him.

ASHLEY sits in the armchair. SASHA perches on the sofa arm.

What are you, you two? Working girls, I take it?

SASHA Oh, yes, we both go to work. Well, my sister does. I just do evenings.

ASHLEY Right. Pin money?

SASHA Sort of. Help pay the rent, you know. In the daytime I'm a student. Catering college. North London.

ASHLEY Where do you work in the evenings?

SASHA The Dorchester.

ASHLEY High class.

SASHA Washing up.

ASHLEY Washing up?

SASHA Girl's got to live.

ASHLEY That's what you were doing tonight, was it? Dressed like that? Washing up?

SASHA I took tonight off. I've been to the opera. Covent Garden.

ASHLEY You don't work from home at all?

SASHA gets up and moves to the table where she finds CHLOË's mobile.

SASHA What? From here? No. Well, my sister sometimes does. Works at home. When she gets a rush job. But that's mainly at weekends.

ASHLEY Weekends?

SASHA Yes, but only if she's – Oh, I see what you mean. You're concerned with you being down below, you mean?

ASHLEY Down below?

SASHA Underneath her. You don't have to worry, she's very quiet. In her line it mainly entails her sitting down. Well, she gets a bit carried away occasionally, jumps about a bit, you know, but – *(Studying the mobile)* Oh, God, look at this! No wonder she got drunk. "Cnt mk it 2nite. Msnt C U agn. Sorry. Z. X." Poor Chloë.

ASHLEY Friend of hers?

SASHA Sort of. Her boyfriend. Zack. Sort of boyfriend, anyway. Isn't that terrible? I keep telling her she should break it off 'cos he doesn't love her, not really, he can't do. Trouble is, I think she loves him. How can someone as clever as she is be so stupid? Can you explain that?

ASHLEY I gave up trying to explain women a long time ago, love.

SASHA Women? Really? Do you find us complicated, do you?

ASHLEY Just a bit.

SASHA I'm not. At least, I don't think I am. I'd like to be because I think complicated people are much more interesting generally, aren't they? I mean Chloë – my sister – she's very complicated and I think that's why people find her interesting. Whereas people don't generally find me interesting, they just find me friendly. Mind you, there's room for both, isn't there? Friendly people and interesting people. There's room for both, isn't there? I mean, I wouldn't actually want to be like Chloë, not at all, if it came down to it. Because the reason she's unhappy a lot of the time is because she's so complicated. Basically, I think I'm happy just to be friendly. But – nothing's ever simple, is it? *(She pauses for breath)*

ASHLEY *(staring at her for a second)* I don't mean to offend you in any way, but I have to say I'm finding you extremely complicated.

SASHA *(smiling)* Really? That's nice. No one's ever said that to me before.

ASHLEY Maybe it's the time of night. You're beginning to make my head ache.

SASHA Oh, I'm sorry. It is very late. Can I get you an aspirin?

ASHLEY *(rising)* No, no, no. I'm going to bed. I need my bed.

SASHA *(smiling)* You and me both.

ASHLEY Well, yes. Perhaps another night, love. No offence.

SASHA *(puzzled)* What?

ASHLEY I'm a bit tired tonight.

SASHA So am I. All on your own down there, are you?

ASHLEY I'm used to it these days, love. I'll survive. *(He stops)* Er – this man you were out with tonight, is he your – er – you know?

SASHA Oh, no. He's just a friend. Heavens, he's old enough to be my father. Practically my grandfather, almost. *(Laughing)* No. We just met – by chance and – we've become friends. That's all.

ASHLEY Good friends?

SASHA If you like. It's a gradually growing friendship.

ASHLEY Is it? He bought you that dress?

SASHA No, I bought it myself. He just – arranged me a discount, that's all.

ASHLEY Helps you with the rent, does he?

SASHA No. We just go out together occasionally. Why are you so interested?

ASHLEY I beg your pardon. It used to be my job. Asking questions. Never got out of the habit.

SASHA What job was that?

ASHLEY I was a policeman.

SASHA *(startled)* A policeman?

ASHLEY Don't panic. Not after you. Retired long ago.

SASHA That's extraordinary! The man I went out with tonight used to be a policeman. Uncle Val used to be a policeman. Years ago.

ASHLEY Uncle Val? Did he now?

SASHA For thirty-four years. He was in the Serious Crime Squad. Which is why he's got knee trouble today.

ASHLEY Amazing.

SASHA Maybe you knew him. What branch were you in?

ASHLEY Serious Crime Squad.

SASHA Really? That's an incredible coincidence, isn't it?

ASHLEY Isn't it just?

SASHA He was a Chief Super.

ASHLEY Was he now?

SASHA What were you?

ASHLEY Detective Sergeant.

SASHA Ah, well. He'd have been senior to you, then, wouldn't he?

ASHLEY He would.

SASHA You probably wouldn't have had much to do with each other, would you?

ASHLEY Not if we could help it.

SASHA I must introduce you. You must both meet. You'd have a lot in common.

ASHLEY I doubt it.

SASHA How long were you in the police, then?

ASHLEY Twenty five years. (*Indicating his eye*) Till I got this. Invalided out. Private security, after that. Desk job.

SASHA How did it happen? Your eye?

ASHLEY High speed car chase. Through Epping Forest. Chasing a stolen security vehicle. Hit a patch of mud. Skidded off the road. Turned over four times. Lucky to be alive. They pulled me out of the wreckage. Propped me against this tree. Left me for dead. I remember coming round and hearing someone say – "This one's a goner, Jim. We can leave him for now, he's a goner."

SASHA How awful. Couldn't you tell them you weren't?

ASHLEY No way. My larynx was frozen with the shock, you see. So in all the confusion, debris and carnage, they assumed me dead. Zipped me up. Took me back in a body bag. I was within an inch of being buried alive. That close. Woke up in the morgue. Screaming. I recovered the use of my vocal chords in the nick of time.

SASHA And that's how you lost your eye?

ASHLEY I lost more than an eye, love.

SASHA Did you?

ASHLEY Suffice it to say, if I was to divest myself in front of you here and now, I'd give you nightmares for the rest of your life.

SASHA My God! What a story.

ASHLEY Ah, well. Those were the days. All different now, of course.

SASHA Yes.

ASHLEY There used to be rules, then. Rules of engagement.

SASHA Honour...

ASHLEY Right. All forgotten these days. Out of the window.

SASHA End of civilisation's just around the corner.

ASHLEY *(looking at her appreciatively)* Right. You've got quite an old head on those young shoulders of yours, haven't you?

SASHA Probably. I'm a bit tired. It's been a long day.

ASHLEY You're a student, you say?

SASHA Yes.

ASHLEY By day, that is. Catering, you say?

SASHA Right. Maybe you can come to dinner. I'll cook you a meal sometime. Seeing as we're neighbours now.

ASHLEY I'd like that very much but I doubt I could afford your prices, love. Not on my pension. Well, goodnight – er –

SASHA *(puzzled)* Sasha. Sasha Vines. I wouldn't charge you for it, you know. I'm only a student. I haven't even qualified yet.

ASHLEY No, that's sweet of you, darling. But if you want to go into the life you've chosen, you take every penny you can get. 'Cos you won't last long.

SASHA Don't you think so?

ASHLEY *(moving to the door)* No way. It'll take its toll.

SASHA My parents are both in the business. They're doing alright.

ASHLEY *(closing his eyes in pain)* God almighty! What a life! Listen Sasha – that's your real name, is it...?

SASHA Of course...

ASHLEY *(confidentially)* ...listen, I know you're probably not able to talk freely, not now but...my name is Ashley and I'm here to help, alright? Not official but you need me, I'm here for you. I've only just met you, but I worry for you, alright? Just remember me. In times of trouble. Ashley Croucher. Remember that name.

SASHA I will. Thank you very much, Mr Croucher.

ASHLEY Ashley. Goodnight then, Sasha.

SASHA Goodnight, Ashley.

ASHLEY *closes the door.* **SASHA** *stands thoughtfully.*

(smiling to herself) People are just so nice.

As she stands, reflecting on this: The lights fade to:

Blackout.

End of Scene Three

Scene Four

*The same. Several days later. It is, again, evening and the
room is in darkness except for the street lighting from
the windows. In a moment, a key in the front door lock
and the sound of* SASHA *and* VAL *laughing.*

SASHA *(as she enters)* ...I didn't mind the paintings, it was those
sculptures that got me. I mean, I wouldn't give them house
room, would you?

VAL Not in my house, certainly.

*SASHA switches on the room lights. She is wearing a
new, fashionable full length coat. They are both carrying
carrier bags, apparently from smart clothing and shoe
shops.*

SASHA And did you – *(Checking round)* I don't think she's
back yet, that's odd – and did you see the price of them?
Unbelievable.

VAL Yes, well, he's a fashionable artist at the moment, that lad.
I used to know his sister. In the old days. She was artistic,
too, in her own way.

SASHA Look at all this stuff. You shouldn't encourage me to
buy all this, Uncle Val, you shouldn't really.

VAL Need to look smart for your new job, won't you?

SASHA You think I got it, then? You think she'll take me on?

VAL 'Course she'll take you on. She was just going through the
motions.

SASHA Be a wonderful job if I get it, wouldn't it? Much better
money and only four nights a week. And then there's the
tips. She told me about the tips.

VAL Oh, yes. You'll get tips. They always get tips.

SASHA And I love the outfit, it's really cute, isn't it? I think I might have to lose a bit of weight, though. I think I might be bulging out a bit in places.

VAL What are you talking about? You'll fill it beautifully.

SASHA Well, I could do with losing a bit. It's your fault. All those meals we keep having. Anyway, if I get it. If. Then all I have to worry about is not getting people's coats muddled up.

VAL I've said, there's no if. The job's yours. She thought you were knockout.

SASHA There were six others, weren't there? And I thought I may have come over as a bit, you know – awkward – with her. With Monique. She seemed so sophisticated.

VAL No, no, no. I've known Mona since she was – well – since she was virtually a kid. Underneath all that, she's a simple working class girl. Broken home. Off the streets. I set her up in that club, you know.

SASHA Did you? I bet that's why she seems so fond of you.

VAL She's good reason to. I saw her alright.

SASHA But then they all do, in their different ways, don't they? I was thinking, on the way home, all these different women, all over London, all owing you so much. There's Gloria in her dress shop. And Rachel in the flower shop. Cheryl with the shoes. Oh, and then there's Debbie in Harrods, I'd forgotten her. And who's the one in Fortnums, again? On the cheese counter?

VAL Lola.

SASHA Lola, that's it. I liked her. And now Monique. Where'd you meet them all? You must have had an address book as big as the bible. I bet you were a devil in your time, Uncle Val, weren't you?

VAL I had my moments. No, I looked after the ones who did right by me, that's all. As was only proper.

SASHA You're an old softy, Uncle Val. I bet you took care of all of them. Even the ones who didn't do right by you.

VAL Oh, I took care of them and all.

SASHA You're a softy, aren't you?

VAL I'd never hurt you, Sasha.

SASHA *(smiling at him)* I know that. I trust you. I trust you more than any man I know. Except possibly my dad. You're a really kind man. Through and through.

VAL *(a little uncomfortable)* Why don't you – get changed Sash? Time's getting on. I'll give you a lift up the Dorchester.

SASHA Could be my last day, couldn't it? *(Reflecting)* It isn't that I didn't have boyfriends before. Back home I had several. You know, proper boyfriends who were usually after something else. But – I don't know – they were nowhere near as much fun as you. *(Gathering up the bags)* Chloë's late. Can't think where she's got to. She's usually home by now. Hope she's alright.

VAL I've told you before, you mustn't worry about her so much. She's a grown woman. She can take care of herself.

SASHA That's the trouble, I don't think she can sometimes. I have to worry a bit. She's my sister.

VAL I don't like to see you worrying. It makes you frown. Every time you think about her, you frown.

SASHA I don't.

VAL Look at you, you're frowning now. I don't like you frowning, Sash. I don't like to see you frowning. It makes me cross to see you frowning.

SASHA Oh, you... Anyway, she's better now. Now she's stopped – you know – thinking about that Zack every twenty seconds. Now he's out of her life, thank God.

VAL Till the next time.

SASHA You know, I was thinking, the nice thing about this new job will be meeting people. I think that's important for me. That I develop my social skills, don't you? I mean, if I'm going to be running my own restaurant, singing and that. I'll need to learn how to talk to people –

The flat doorbell rings.

(going to the door) Who's that then? Can't be Chloë, she's got her key.

SASHA *opens the door. It is* ASHLEY.

Oh, hallo, Ashley. Haven't seen you for a bit. Settling in alright?

ASHLEY *(gravely)* May I come in for a minute, Sasha?

SASHA 'Course. Come in.

She stands aside. ASHLEY *enters and sees* VAL. *They stare at each other.*

Ashley, this is Uncle Val – not really my Uncle but I call him that – Val, this is Ashley who's just moved in downstairs.

VAL How do you do?

ASHLEY *(coolly)* How do you do?

SASHA You've got a lot in common, you two. You're not going to believe this, Val, but Ashley was actually –

ASHLEY Sasha, sorry to interrupt. But I've got a bit of news that I think you ought to know about first.

SASHA News?

ASHLEY Bad news, I'm afraid.

SASHA It's not my parents, is it? Nothing's happened to them, has it?

ASHLEY No, they're fine, Sasha, so far as I know. No, it's –

SASHA Chloë. It's Chloë, isn't it? Oh, nothing's happened to Chloë, please –?

ASHLEY Just – give me a second, Sasha. It's not Chloë, either. She's just gone to the hospital –

SASHA Hospital? Oh God, why's she in hospital...? What's she doing in the hospital?

ASHLEY *(loudly, drowning her)* She's just gone to the hospital to see her boyfriend! *(More quietly now he has her attention)* She's gone to visit – Zack, is it –?

SASHA Zack, yes.

ASHLEY – and she asked me to tell you when you came in. Seeing as you forgot to switch on your answering machine and you don't have a mobile.

VAL You need a mobile, Sasha, I keep telling you, you need a mobile.

SASHA What's wrong with Zack?

ASHLEY He was – he was mugged apparently. Assaulted.

SASHA Oh, no!

ASHLEY Two blokes. He was coming through the alley from where he works to the car park. They jumped him.

SASHA Was he hurt? Did they steal anything?

ASHLEY *(awkwardly)* They – er – got his mobile phone apparently...

SASHA Oh, well. Could have been worse.

ASHLEY No, I haven't finished. They got his mobile off him and they – this is a bit delicate, this is – they inserted it. If you follow.

SASHA Inserted it?

ASHLEY Into him. If you follow.

SASHA *(realising)* Oh, God!

ASHLEY Fortunately, with the advance of modern technology, the instruments are considerably smaller than they used to be – but – nonetheless – extremely painful. I would imagine.

VAL Nasty.

SASHA Horrible.

ASHLEY They rushed him straight to St Thomas's where they performed a successful emergency operation. That's where Chloë is now.

SASHA Is Zack alright?

ASHLEY Bit shaken. Slight loss of dignity, I imagine. Worst bit was that, whilst they were operating, his phone started ringing. You know – from within.

SASHA Him?

ASHLEY Several times. Apparently. I believe a nurse answered it as soon as it became – accessible. Turned out to be your sister calling.

SASHA Poor Chloë.

VAL *is making strange sounds in his throat.*

I'd better go and give her some support. She'll need someone. *(Noticing* VAL*)* You alright, Uncle Val?

VAL *(dabbing his eyes)* Yes, I just got – something in my eye. I'll run you up there, Sasha, if you like.

SASHA Thank you. *(Indicating her carrier bags)* I'll just – get rid of these. Won't be a second.

SASHA *goes off to the bedroom. Silence.*

VAL You've moved in downstairs, I see?

ASHLEY I'm never far behind you, Val. Like I promised you. *(Pause)* I hear you joined the force?

VAL Just in passing.

ASHLEY I know these are desperate times, Val, but I think the Met has still got some way to sink before they recruit you.

VAL Really? I thought I'd fit in rather well these days.

Pause.

ASHLEY That wouldn't have anything to do with you, I suppose? What you found so hilarious. The misplacing of that luckless man's mobile phone?

VAL I don't go around doing things like that. Not any more. You know that, Ashley. *(Pause)* Not a bad idea though. There's one or two people I know are eligible for that. But don't look at me. I've retired.

ASHLEY Well, I haven't retired, Val. I'm still on the case.

VAL Fifty years, Ashley. What you got? One parking fine. Come on! Why don't you give it up, mate? Go to Bournemouth and blow your pension.

ASHLEY I'll find someone to testify, don't worry. One of your warped little family, perhaps. They must be getting fairly pissed off with you by now. Spending their ill gotten fortune on assorted young women. One of them even tried to run you over, didn't they?

VAL Internal matter, speedily dealt with. Anything I'm spending is mine. I earnt it, I'm spending it.

ASHLEY No, Val. You didn't earn a penny of it, that's the point. It's your girls who earned it for you. Giving up the best years of their lives. Horizontally. So you can swan about in five hundred quid suits in a bloody custom built Roller.

VAL This suit cost more than that, sunshine. I saw my girls alright. That's why you can't get them to testify.

ASHLEY The ones who survived, anyway.

VAL You've no evidence of that. You say that out loud, I'll have you.

ASHLEY And what's more, you leave this little girl alone. Don't you start your nasty, evil ways with her. Not one hair of her head.

VAL Why should I harm her? She's befriended me in my old age.

ASHLEY Befriended? People like you don't have friends, Val. Your hands have been that deep in shit for so long, anyone you touch they finish up as filthy and greedy and twisted as you are.

They glare at each other.

VAL We'll see about that, won't we?

SASHA *returns. She has changed her clothes.*

SASHA Sorry to keep you. You both been catching up?

VAL Catching up, yes.

SASHA Right! Better be off. Sure it's OK to run me there, Uncle Val?

VAL Your wish is my command, my dear. You can phone them at your work from the car.

SASHA *(to* ASHLEY*)* Isn't he the best Uncle? Ever? Off we go, then.

VAL *(opening the door for her)* After you!

SASHA *(going out)* Thank you.

SASHA *goes off ahead of them both.*

VAL *(mockingly to* ASHLEY*)* After you, Ashley.

ASHLEY *(turning as he goes, softly)* Not one hair. Or I will, I swear. I'll kill you.

ASHLEY *goes off.* VAL *turns and looks at the room, smiling to himself.*

SASHA *(offstage, calling)* Uncle Val!

VAL   Coming, my dear, just coming. *(Looking around one last time, softly to himself)* This place could do with some proper furniture and all.

VAL *switches off the light and closes the front door. As he does so:*

A blackout.

End of Act I

ACT II

Scene One

A few weeks later. Noon.

The same flat though now transformed by **VAL**'s *gift of 'proper furniture'.*

A new carpet, sofa, armchair, coffee table, dining table, chairs, sideboard and a replacement high tech desk for **CHLOË**. *The overall effect is a bit 'designed' and although far more glossy (not to say garishly expensive) than its former self, the room is devoid of real character and seemingly uninhabited.*

SASHA *comes from the bedrooms. She, too, has had something of a makeover since we last saw her. Her clothes are all decidedly designer, her hair, makeup and general grooming are, like the room she stands in, expensive, chic, yet ultimately in danger of removing all her individuality.*

She surveys the room with an anxious eye. Everything has to be just right. From the kitchen an effortful grunt from **ASHLEY**.

SASHA *(calling to* **ASHLEY***)* Are you managing?

Another grunt from the kitchen.

(anxiously) Do be careful, Uncle Ashley.

ASHLEY *(offstage)* That's done it!

SASHA *(calling)* Have you done it?

ASHLEY *(offstage)* Done it!

SASHA Well done!

> **ASHLEY** *comes on from the kitchen. He is wearing overalls. He is slightly breathless and starting to wheeze slightly.*

ASHLEY *(breathlessly)* Done it!

SASHA You alright? You haven't overdone it?

ASHLEY Fine. Just get my breath.

SASHA You've got to be careful at your age. Sit down.

ASHLEY No, they'd put it about 3 mil too far to the right, you see. Which is why you couldn't get the door open properly. It just needed a shove.

SASHA You should have waited. I'd have got someone round. They're heavy, those freezers.

ASHLEY You can say that again.

SASHA You! There's no stopping you, is there? You just plunge straight in.

ASHLEY Needs to be done. Got to be ready, haven't you? Got to look perfect for her, hasn't it?

SASHA It does. It looks perfect. I hardly like to sit down, it all looks so perfect. I don't know how I'm ever going to use that kitchen. Can't bear the thought of getting that stove dirty. *(Looking round again, anxiously)* I hope she'll approve.

ASHLEY 'Course she will.

SASHA Incidentally. Just before she went on holiday, I meant to say, she said that when she first met you, you mistook her for a prostitute.

ASHLEY *(awkwardly)* Ah, yes. Well.

SASHA What made you think she was a prostitute? She was quite upset.

ASHLEY I know she was.

SASHA What on earth made you think she was a prostitute?

ASHLEY It was a – result of an early misunderstanding. When I first came up to help you with her that night.

SASHA *(digesting this)* Oh. I see. *(She reflects)* Did you think I was a prostitute as well, then?

ASHLEY Initially. *(Anxiously)* Sorry. Have I upset you, now?

SASHA No. *(Slight pause)* I'm not.

ASHLEY No, I know you're not. Now.

SASHA Strange thing to think though, isn't it? Do you go around doing a lot of that sort of thing?

ASHLEY No. It was just in that instance – The company you were in – with Val. I jumped to a conclusion. He's not a good person, Sasha, I keep trying to tell you, he's an evil man –

SASHA *(rising and moving away, sharply)* I said, I don't want to hear –

ASHLEY But there are things about him you should know –

SASHA I've told you I don't want to hear bad things about my friends –

ASHLEY Would you just listen for one –?

SASHA – I'm not listening! If you're going to say bad things about him, you can just leave now, Ashley. I'm not joking. You want to stay friends with me, then you respect my friends. I'm sure you've done wrong things in your life. I'm sure you have. But Val never tells tales about you, does he? Where my friends are concerned, the past stays the past? Alright?

ASHLEY I hope you know what you're doing.

SASHA Everybody keeps saying that. I know exactly what I'm doing. I'm having a really good time, that's what I'm doing.

ASHLEY All I'm saying is that sooner or later someone might present you with the bill, that's all.

SASHA *(smiling)* Now you sound like my sister. *(Suddenly worried)* I hope she approves. You think she'll approve?

ASHLEY Bound to, isn't she?

SASHA You never know with Chloë. I had this terrible dream last night, she walked in, took one look and went completely hairless. Just stood there screaming, what have you done? Get it out! Get it all out!

ASHLEY She won't do that. It's beautiful. Quality. Like a show room. You could have people walking round in here.

SASHA *(laughing)* Go on!

ASHLEY Put up a rope, charge admission.

SASHA Silly!

ASHLEY No, seriously, you've got taste, Sasha. Everything in here says taste.

SASHA It says money, anyway. But to be fair, I did get help, didn't I? From Charmaine. I mean, she advised me. Found the items.

ASHLEY Ah, but you made the final choice, didn't you?

SASHA Oh, yes, I made the final choice. Charmaine chose, but the final choice was mine. She was very helpful, though. You want a cup of tea or something?

ASHLEY No, I must get downstairs. It's nearly time, isn't it?

SASHA Oh, yes. So it is.

ASHLEY If the plane's not delayed.

SASHA No, I checked this morning. It was due to take off on time.

ASHLEY Has she been in touch at all? Were they having a good time?

SASHA She sent a card but that was only on day two. They were still together on day two. Zack hadn't walked out by then. Mind you, I don't think he could have walked far, even if he'd wanted to, not in his condition, poor thing. But they seemed to be having a good time back then. But I suppose in two weeks, anything can happen. Can with those two.

ASHLEY Majorca.

SASHA Yes. Ever been there, have you?

ASHLEY Only once. On business.

SASHA Nice was it?

ASHLEY I don't know. All I saw was the inside of the police station in Palma.

SASHA Oh.

ASHLEY Had to bring this bloke back. Wife murderer. Decapitated her. Buried her in a gravel pit near Oakhampton.

SASHA Goodness. You've certainly seen life, haven't you, Uncle Ashley?

ASHLEY Enough to know its dangers. Like I say, Sasha, you take care. Always be on your guard. Sometimes, you're too trusting. In this world, nobody gives you anything for nothing, remember that.

SASHA You have.

ASHLEY I've what?

SASHA You've done all this for me for nothing. Helped move things. Put up the pictures. Fixed the curtain rail...

ASHLEY Well, maybe I was – I wanted to keep an eye on you, that's all.

SASHA Then I've got nothing to worry about, have I? With people like you and Uncle Val to look after me, what harm am I going to come to, eh?

ASHLEY *(studying her)* Yes. Maybe you're right. I hope so. *(At the window)* There's a taxi just pulling up. This must be her.

SASHA Oh, God. Right. I meant to put the kettle on.

ASHLEY *(moving to the door)* I'll be off. See you later. I don't think she'll want to see me. She still isn't talking to me. She'll love it, Sasha...

SASHA *(rather anxiously)* Yes.

ASHLEY Don't worry.

ASHLEY *goes out.*

SASHA *straightens one or two things that don't need straightening and waits.*

A key in the flat's front door. It opens. CHLOË *appears, slightly sun-tanned. Due to having a number of packages, duty free bags, suitcases, etc., she enters backwards and so doesn't immediately notice the room.*

CHLOË *(struggling)* Shit!

She eventually achieves her objective and gets all her luggage through the door. This she now closes. CHLOË *finally turns and sees* SASHA.

I've got so much...stuff...

Silence. She stares at the room. Taking it all in. Her gaze surveys each wall, each item in turn. It takes a very long time for it to sink in. She is, at first, merely stunned. Her true reaction will follow shortly.

SASHA Do you approve?

CHLOË *(stunned)* We've moved, haven't we? When did we move?

SASHA No, it's the same flat. I just – improved it, a bit – I think.

CHLOË What have you done, Sasha? What have you done to our home?

SASHA I just changed one or two...

CHLOË I cannot believe this. I simply cannot believe this. Where's my desk?

SASHA There.

CHLOË That is not my desk. In no way is that my desk.

SASHA It's a new one.

CHLOË What are you talking about, a new one? It doesn't even look like a desk. How could you do this? Sasha, how could you do this to me?

SASHA You don't approve?

CHLOË Approve? It's like the front room of a bloody brothel. It's vile. It's revolting! It's repellent.

SASHA Perhaps you'll prefer the kitchen?

CHLOË The kitchen? You've done this to the kitchen, as well?

SASHA I put a few new things in.

CHLOË *(marching to the kitchen door)* This has got to be a joke!

CHLOË *goes off to the kitchen, briefly.*

SASHA *(calling after her)* It needed things doing to it. That cold tap kept dripping for a start, didn't it?

CHLOË *(off, with a cry)* Oh, dear God!

CHLOË *returns.*

What have you done to my kitchen? What have you done to my bloody kitchen?

SASHA Our kitchen.

CHLOË No. <u>Your</u> kitchen now. I'm never setting foot in there again. Ever.

SASHA You don't like that either?

CHLOË If there's one thing I loathe more than anything else, it's bloody stainless steel. It's like a hall of mirrors. It's hideous, Sasha. Just hideous. How could you do this without even consulting me? How could you do it? No, this is a joke, isn't it? Please, tell me it's a joke. We're on some terrible

TV programme. In a minute, appalling people are going to come leaping out of cupboards, aren't they? How could you do this to me, Sasha?

SASHA *(unhappily)* Well... *(Her eyes move almost inadvertently in the direction of the bedroom)*

CHLOË *(following her gaze)* You haven't done the bedrooms as well. Please tell me you haven't done the bedrooms?

SASHA Just one or two little improvements...

CHLOË My bedroom? You've done my bedroom, too, haven't you? I don't even <u>allow</u> people into my bedroom and you've gone and done my bedroom.

CHLOË *goes off to the bedrooms.*

SASHA *(calling after her)* They were very careful not to disturb your things more than they...had to.

Offstage, CHLOË *screams.*

CHLOË *(with a terrible cry)* I cannot believe this. I just cannot believe this. What is this on the walls? What is it? What is it?

SASHA *(grumpily)* Fur. It's only fur.

SASHA *waits unhappily. She is becoming rather tearful.*

Another scream offstage.

What have you done to my bathroom?

SASHA *(to herself, muttering)* Our bathroom...

CHLOË *returns.*

CHLOË Well, it is. It's a brothel, isn't it? You've turned the place into a brothel, haven't you? I certainly can't sleep in there. I'm surprised you haven't stuck a mirror on my ceiling and had done with it!

SASHA We couldn't. The ceiling wasn't strong enough to take it.

CHLOË We? Who's we? You and that bloody Uncle Val presumably.

SASHA No, it was a proper designer. I had a proper designer in. We did it so we could surprise you...

CHLOË You had a <u>designer</u> do this? What designer?

SASHA Charmaine.

CHLOË <u>Charmaine</u>?

SASHA Yes.

CHLOË *(furiously)* Where did you find her? From a card in a phone box? Well, you tell Charmaine that I want everything back as it was or I am suing her for every penny she's got. I want my tatty old desk. I want my armchair with the wobbly leg. I want my old fashioned chipped bath, not that plastic monstrosity full of holes and most of all I want my own bed. You tell her that from me!

SASHA I can't get it all back. It's probably on the tip by now.

CHLOË Well get your sugar daddy to hire a truck and get it back. In the meantime, I'm leaving, Sasha, I'm staying in a hotel until this is sorted out, do you hear? *(She starts to gather up her things)*

SASHA I think you're being very unfair.

CHLOË What?

SASHA I've gone to a lot of trouble with this. I thought you'd be pleased. I did this as much for you, you know.

CHLOË No, Sasha, let's get this straight, in no way did you do this for me. You did this entirely for you, dear. God knows what's going on in your personal life, I dread to think, but you're starting to behave just like that dirty old man.

SASHA *(angrily)* He's not a dirty old man, don't you dare call him that!

CHLOË *(slightly alarmed at the outburst)* Alright, I'm sorry –

SASHA He's just fond of me. He hasn't touched me. He hasn't laid a finger on me.

CHLOË Sasha, he's destroying you. Can't you see it? Look at you, girl. He's changing you, turning you into something you're not. God, I've only been away two weeks and look at you. He's spending money on you like water. I don't know what he's after but he's gradually destroying you.

SASHA (*sulkily*) Like water? What are you talking about. It's all my money.

CHLOË You bought all this with your money?

SASHA More or less.

CHLOË Sasha, there's about ten thousand quids' worth of stuff in the kitchen alone.

SASHA Well, he knows where to get things cheap, that's all.

CHLOË (*staring at her*) And you really believe that, do you?

SASHA (*evasively*) Yes.

Slight pause.

CHLOË You might be a naïve kid from the country, Sasha, but I don't think you're that much of a fool. You may not have paid for this now but you'll pay for it eventually, I promise you that, dear. You always do.

SASHA *glowers at her.*

CHLOË *produces a gift-wrapped package from one of her bags.*

(*placing the package on the table*) Here. A present from Majorca. You might as well have it. Nice little piece of local pottery. Though God knows where you're going to put it in here. Good-bye, then.

SASHA (*with growing fury, quietly at first*) You're just jealous, aren't you? Got a boyfriend, treats you like dirt, has you trotting around after him like a bloody little dog, here girl, good girl, beg girl, roll over. Pathetic! Woman of your age. No

wonder you're half falling apart. Pathetic! No wonder people
laugh at you. Behind your back. Laughing at you, you're
so pathetic. And then you see me getting people running
after me. Treating me like I was special and you can't stand
it, can you? Ignorant little country girl, me! And look at
me now, eh? You know how much this necklace cost, you
know how much this bracelet was? You couldn't afford it
in a bloody year, girl, I can tell you. And you just can't bear
the thought of it, can you? Getting older and older, more
washed out, and you're never going to make it now, are you?
Bloody second rate failure, you! Majorca? Bloody Majorca?
Pathetic! Know who goes to Majorca, then, do you? Bloody
second rate bloody failures like you go to Majorca, that's who
goes to Majorca. Me, bloody Pacific Ocean, mate, private
yacht or nothing, me, I tell you. Well, go on then! Off you
go! You want to go and sulk in a poky little bloody hotel
on your own, you go! Go on, you bugger off! See if I care!
Go on, get out! Get out!

SASHA *stands, breathless from this outburst.* CHLOË, *very
shaken, opens the front door, gathers up her belongings
and, without another word, goes out.* SASHA *watches her.
Impetuously, she snatches up the gift-wrapped present
and goes to the front door.*

(*yelling after* CHLOË) And take your stupid, cheap, fucking
Majorcan present with you!

SASHA *hurls the package into the hall. We hear it shatter
against the wall.* SASHA *returns and closes the door.*

*She stands in the room trying to contain her anger,
breathing heavily.*

(*after a moment, muttering to herself*) Me, I only have
expensive things in here.

As she stands, still recovering, the lights fade to:

Blackout.

End of Scene One

Scene Two

The same. A few days later.

The place is very much as it was in the previous scene. But perhaps there is actually more sign now that it is actually inhabited.

The new table is laid rather elaborately for dinner for four.

VAL is at the table, fitting some fresh candles into a new candle holder. The new hi-fi is softly playing classical music.

In a moment, SASHA comes out of the kitchen.

She is evidently in the midst of dinner preparations. She is wearing an apron over her new dress. She looks, if anything, even more glossy than before. She stops and watches VAL as he completes his task.

SASHA They look good.

VAL They do. Good purchase of yours.

SASHA Nice to eat at home for once. Christen the new place. I mean, I love restaurants but...

VAL This is nice, too. How are things out there?

SASHA Under control. Just. Still getting the hang of that stove, rather. So high tech. Knobs and levers, all different programmes. Need a science degree to work it.

VAL Well, you'll have that soon, won't you?

SASHA How do you mean?

VAL Another year at your college. Qualified for anything then, aren't you?

SASHA I suppose. Missed so many days recently, it's amazing I remember how to cook at all.

VAL Did I tell you? Tonight you look drop dead gorgeous.

SASHA Thank you. *(Smiling)* I love the way you do that. Tell me I look nice. You always do that. Even when I look a mess, you say it.

VAL You never look a mess.

SASHA Oh, no? Still, I love it. Nice to be appreciated. Some men, they never say it, do they? You practically have to say it for them. "Don't I look lovely this evening, Jim?" "Oh, yes dear, so you do. Now I come to look at you." You want a glass of wine before they come?

VAL Why not?

SASHA I'll get it. White?

VAL Yes, I can do it. In the fridge is it?

SASHA Yes, on the shelf. I opened it. It's that Pulooney Maltrashet, is that alright?

VAL *(as he goes)* Sounds good to me.

SASHA *waits and surveys the room.*

SASHA *(calling)* All these weeks. I've never once cooked you a meal, have I? I'm a bit nervous.

VAL *(offstage)* Smells delicious already.

SASHA *(calling)* I hardly started cooking yet.

She studies the room some more.

(frowning) You don't think this is bad taste, do you?

VAL *(offstage)* What?

SASHA This room. It's not bad taste, is it?

VAL *(offstage)* 'Course it's not in bad taste. You know how much that sofa cost for starters?

SASHA Right. I don't think it's bad taste. Not at all. She was talking rubbish.

VAL *returns with two glasses of white wine.*

VAL Who?

SASHA That sister of mine. Really upset me, she did. After all the trouble I went to. *(Taking her glass)* Really ungrateful.

VAL Don't frown! Good health.

SASHA Sorry. *(She smiles)* Cheers!

They drink.

VAL Beautiful. Like velvet that, isn't it? Thirty-four quid a bottle.

SASHA *(frowning again)* I chose that desk specially for her.

VAL Sash, leave it alone. We've been over it. I've told you, you mustn't let it keep upsetting you, must you? Because if people upset you, they upset me. And you wouldn't want to see me cross now, would you?

SASHA *(smiling)* You never get cross.

VAL *(jokily)* Oh, you'd be surprised. You haven't seen me. Whoo-hoo!

SASHA *(giggling)* Whoo-hoo! I don't think you know how to be cross.

VAL *(affectionately)* Not with you, Sash. Never with you, girl.

SASHA You're such a lovely person. Everything I ask for. Practically.

VAL Practically.

SASHA And things I never asked for. Things I never even thought of asking for. You're so generous to me.

VAL Gives me pleasure just watching your face. Like a kid at Christmas.

SASHA Remember? First time I met you. Father Christmas, weren't you? My own personal Father Christmas, you are.

VAL You told me you used to believe in him.

SASHA I still do. (*She smiles at him*) You don't mind me asking these people tonight, do you?

VAL It's your party, Sash. Invite who you like.

SASHA I sometimes think you don't like sharing me. You want me all to yourself.

VAL I do. I'm greedy.

SASHA Still. I thought I owed Charmaine. She's been just brilliant. Organising all this in two weeks.

VAL Yes, Charmaine's alright.

SASHA And I did promise Unc – Ashley a meal. He was such a help.

VAL Oh, yes?

SASHA He was! Oh, you! You really don't like him, do you? I don't know what he's ever done to you.

VAL He's never done anything to me.

SASHA It's like he poisoned your pet hamster or something when you were kids.

VAL So long as he doesn't hang around here too much.

SASHA I don't see him that often. Just occasionally I do. I can't avoid it. He can't help living downstairs, can he?

VAL Just don't get too friendly with him, that's all.

SASHA He seems nice enough to me. He was a policeman, wasn't he?

VAL You're a trusting person, Sasha. You see the best in everyone, you do. All the brass monkeys rolled into one, you are.

SASHA I'm not that stupid. I know you think I am sometimes.

VAL You wouldn't know evil if it came up and stared you in the face.

From the kitchen, a timer starts beeping.

SASHA Oh, that'll be the oven. Just heating it up for the canapés. I made some canapés.

VAL I'll tell you something about him. He was never even a policeman.

SASHA Who?

VAL Ashley.

SASHA That's odd. That's what he said about you. That you were never a policeman.

VAL Did he? What else did he say?

SASHA I don't want to talk about him. He's a friend. All he said was you were a bad influence on me. I said, I knew that. That's why I loved you.

SASHA goes off. The beeping stops.

VAL *(softly)* Did he now?

The flat doorbell rings.

SASHA *(offstage)* Oh, no. It's all happening. Could you get that please?

VAL *(calling)* I'm going. *(To himself)* I wonder who this can be?

VAL opens the front door. ASHLEY is there.

Well, well. It's the eagle eye of the law.

ASHLEY *(sourly)* No need to get personal. I haven't even got through the bloody door yet, have I?

VAL *(expansively)* Come in! Come in!

ASHLEY I thought this evening was supposed to be a truce?

VAL It is. I apologise, Ashley. That was a cheap jibe.

ASHLEY It was indeed. But then I've no doubt you get your jibes at a discount, along with everything else in life.

VAL *(admonishingly)* Ah! Ah! Ah!

SASHA *(offstage)* Is that Ashley?

ASHLEY *(calling)* Evening, Sasha!

SASHA *(offstage)* Be with you in a minute, Ashley. Just warming the canapés. Will you offer Ashley some wine, Uncle Val?

VAL *(elaborately politely)* Would you care for a glass of wine, Ashley?

ASHLEY *(likewise)* I'd love some, Uncle Val. A glass of white if I may.

VAL *(calling)* He'll have a glass of white, Sash. Can you bring one with you when you come?

SASHA *(offstage)* Won't be a sec.

ASHLEY *(studying the table)* Who else are we expecting? That interior designer, I take it?

VAL Sasha's invited Charmaine, yes. As a thank you.

ASHLEY Charmaine. Yes, I did meet her briefly. When she was round here. One of yours, I take it?

VAL She's one of my protégés, yes.

ASHLEY Protégés. That's a new word for it. Particularly good when it comes to bedroom ceilings, I imagine.

VAL Ashley, one more word like that and you're straight out that door.

ASHLEY Alright. I apologise, in turn.

VAL This is Sasha's evening. We make it work for her, alright? We're her guests, she invited us, we behave ourselves. Ground rules. What's between us, is between us two. It's old ground. Nothing to do with her.

ASHLEY *(grudgingly)* Right.

VAL Tonight is armistice day.

    SASHA *enters with two glasses. She has temporarily removed her apron.*

SASHA Here we are. Hallo, Ashley.

ASHLEY Ah, thank you. That looks welcome. You're looking very lovely tonight, Sasha.

SASHA *(kissing* **ASHLEY** *on the cheek)* Thank you.

ASHLEY Absolutely beautiful.

VAL Yes, isn't she. I was just saying that before you arrived.

ASHLEY Exquisite.

VAL Out of this world, isn't she?

ASHLEY Little bit of heaven.

VAL You can say that again.

SASHA *(a little overwhelmed by this)* Thank you. Well. Cheers!

VAL Cheers!

ASHLEY Good health.

Silence.

Very nice.

SASHA Pulooney Maltrashet. Montrash...

VAL Puligny Montrachet.

SASHA Pulig... Puli... I can never say it, can I? I can drink it. I just can't say it. *(She laughs)*

The men laugh.

VAL Big day this, Ashley.

ASHLEY How come?

VAL First time we'll be sampling her cooking isn't it, Sash?

SASHA I hope you'll like it.

ASHLEY I'm sure we will.

VAL She's been hard at it all day, haven't you? Shopping. Preparing. Nonstop, apparently.

ASHLEY I know. I helped her with some of the shopping.

VAL Did you?

SASHA Just up the stairs there.

VAL You shouldn't have done that, Ashley. You get Frankie to do that, Sasha.

SASHA Well. Ashley offered, so –

VAL That's what he's there for, Frankie. At your beck and call. He did drive you down the supermarket, I take it?

SASHA Oh, yes. And he pushed the trolley round. He's very helpful. He doesn't ever say much but he's very helpful.

VAL Strong silent type. *(To* **ASHLEY***)* My nephew Frankie.

ASHLEY Yes, I do recall him. I think he and I had dealings at some stage.

VAL Well, he was a wild lad. In his youth.

ASHLEY Runs in the family, then.

VAL *(laughing)* Probably.

They all laugh. Silence.

SASHA I don't know where Charmaine's got to.

ASHLEY Maybe the traffic.

SASHA I could ring her. On my new mobile. It's amazing. The latest model, Ashley.

ASHLEY Amazing.

SASHA She must be able to find the place, she's been here enough times. *(Pause)* So long as she's not too late. Or the dinner'll spoil.

VAL *(darkly)* She'd better not be, for her sake.

Pause.

ASHLEY How's your sister, Sasha? How's Chloë? Have you heard from her?

VAL *(scowling)* Don't for God's sake mention Chloë.

SASHA I haven't for days. She came back once for some clothes but that's all.

VAL She's gone, she's forgotten. We don't mention her again in this house, not ever.

SASHA *(meekly)* No.

The front door buzzer sounds.

Oh, this must be her.

SASHA *goes to the entry phone and answers.*

(calling) Hi! Come on up! *(She goes and opens the flat door)*

CHARMAINE *(offstage)* So sorry I'm late, Sasha dear. I got delayed.

SASHA You're not late. Come on. Come up and have a drink.

CHARMAINE *appears. She is probably in her late fifties or early sixties but it is hard to tell. Her appearance is somewhat exotic, even eccentric. Her figure, long since gone to seed, is draped with layers of clothing, her hair a defiant red and her makeup excessive.*

CHARMAINE *(as she enters)* That is music to my ears, dear, music to my – Val!

VAL Charmaine! How're you keeping?

VAL *and* **CHARMAINE** *embrace like old friends.*

CHARMAINE It's my dearest, most precious man in the world. In the whole world. I love this man. I love this man best. I'm sorry, Sasha. I adore him.

SASHA I'll get you a drink. White wine? *(She hesitates but gets no reply)*

SASHA *returns to the kitchen.*

VAL How you keeping, then? Alright, Charmaine?

CHARMAINE Oh, I've never felt better in all my life, you know. It's eerie. I keep waiting, thinking any day now something's got to give, something vital's going to pack in. But it hasn't so far. I just keep going. *(To* ASHLEY*)* Hallo, we've met before, haven't we?

VAL This is Ashley from downstairs.

ASHLEY Downstairs.

CHARMAINE Ashley downstairs, that's right.

VAL I'll take your coat, shall I, Charmaine?

CHARMAINE Oh, ta. *(As she removes her coat)* Nice to meet you again, Ashley, how are you keeping, downstairs?

ASHLEY I'm keeping well, thank you.

CHARMAINE Good, that's the way. You're looking well, Val. You're looking well.

VAL I'm pretty well, yes. Considering.

CHARMAINE Don't you think he's looking well, Ashley?

VAL Yes, he's looking well, yes.

CHARMAINE He's lucky, he's got that sort of skin, hasn't he? But I think we're all looking well, considering.

VAL Considering, yes.

CHARMAINE Lucky to be alive, really.

ASHLEY Some of us are.

> SASHA *returns with a glass of wine.*

CHARMAINE Oh, thank you, dear. That's just what I needed. Oh, you look a picture, Sasha. A real picture, doesn't she? I wish I had a camera. Doesn't she look a picture, Val?

VAL I think she does.

ASHLEY She does.

SASHA Thank you.

CHARMAINE You just want to hang her on the wall and frame her, don't you? I used to have a figure like that when I was her age, didn't I, Val?

SASHA You've still got a figure.

CHARMAINE Oh, not any more, dear, not any more. *(To* ASHLEY*)* How's your eye these days, Ashley?

ASHLEY My eye?

CHARMAINE Is it any better?

ASHLEY No. I lost it.

CHARMAINE Lost it?

ASHLEY It's gone. In an accident.

SASHA Ashley was in a high speed car chase in Epping Forest. He turned over four times. Didn't you?

ASHLEY *(with a glance at* VAL*)* More or less.

CHARMAINE Now, before I do anything else, I must take a look. I want to see it now it's all being lived in. I want to see how it's responding to being lived in. Do you mind, Sasha?

SASHA Please...

CHARMAINE *(studying the room)* Yes...mmmm...yes. It all seems much more mellow now, doesn't it? Mellower. Now that it's actually inhabited. A room always reacts to being lived in... *(Feeling the furniture)* Yes, we did do right with these textures didn't we, Sasha? Feel that texture, Val. I adore the sheer feel of that. I could go to bed and curl up with that. *(Moving to the kitchen)* Do you mind, Sasha...?

SASHA Go ahead...

CHARMAINE *and* SASHA *go off to the kitchen.*

VAL Epping Forest? It was a drunken darts match in Dagenham, wasn't it? High speed car chase. On your bicycle were you?

ASHLEY Shut up! You don't deserve this, you know. Women falling all over you.

VAL Oh, come on, Ashley. They'd be falling all over you if you weren't such a miserable sod.

ASHLEY I've good reason to be miserable, the way life's treated me.

VAL Come on, lighten up.

CHARMAINE *and* SASHA *return.*

CHARMAINE ...yes, I think that works. Do you find it works?

SASHA Yes, it's perfect. I may just have to move one or two of the –

CHARMAINE Oh, I meant to ask, how's your sister? Chloë, is it?

SASHA She's well. She's – away at the moment.

CHARMAINE I was dying to know how she'd react. When she saw the place? How did she react? Did she approve?

SASHA *(with a glance at* VAL*)* She was – knocked out.

CHARMAINE I bet she was. *(In the bedroom doorway)* Do you mind, Sasha?

SASHA No, please. Sorry, I don't think I've made the bed...

SASHA *follows* CHARMAINE *off to the bedrooms.*

ASHLEY What have I got to lighten up about? My wife walked out on me –

VAL She walked out on you because you were such a miserable bastard.

ASHLEY It was the pressure of my work. That's what drove her away. Thanks to crooked little villains like you...

VAL You should've taken the day off, occasionally. That's your problem, Ashley, you can't enjoy leisure. Look at you, you've

been out of the force thirty years and you still can't take
a break!

ASHLEY I'll take a break, the day I put you behind bars.

VAL Then I have news for you, you'll be working till the day
you drop, sunbeam.

> **CHARMAINE** *returns with* **SASHA** *still following.*

CHARMAINE Well, I'm glad she likes her bedroom. It's just
a shame we couldn't get that mirror up on the ceiling. It
would have just finished it off, wouldn't it?

SASHA Yes, it probably would. I'll just get the canapés.

> **SASHA** *goes off to the kitchen.*

CHARMAINE Canapés. Oh. She's a bright girl isn't she, Val?

VAL She is.

CHARMAINE Shiny as a little button. She's so lucky to have all
this, isn't she? You're a generous person, Val, you really are.
I hope she realises how lucky she is. I mean I hope she's
appreciative.

VAL In her own way.

CHARMAINE But she shows her appreciation, Val? In return?
That's what I mean.

VAL She gives me happiness, Charmaine. That's what she gives
me. She gives me hours of joy watching her walking around,
watching her speak, hearing her laugh. How she reacts to
things. Spontaneously. She's a true innocent. And she's
full of wonder. I'm over seventy years old. Charmaine, and
here I am partaking that wonder all over again. I'm a very
fortunate man.

ASHLEY *(muttering)* You can say that again.

CHARMAINE *(a little moved)* Well I hope she never disappoints
you, Val. Doesn't let you down.

VAL How could she ever do that? Look at her.

SASHA returns with a plate of home-made canapés. Aware she's being talked about, she looks at them shyly.

SASHA I hope these have turned out alright. It's the first time I've made them.

CHARMAINE Oh, they look delicious. Scrumptious!

SASHA Wait! I forgot the plates! Sideplates!

VAL It's alright, it doesn't matter, Sash, we'll eat them in our fingers. It's alright.

SASHA Sure?

CHARMAINE Save washing up.

VAL I'll fetch some more wine.

SASHA I can do it.

VAL No, you sit for a minute. You're the hostess. You sit and entertain your guests, Sash.

SASHA *(calling)* There's still some left and there's a new bottle if you need it.

VAL goes off to the kitchen. Pause.

CHARMAINE So, Sasha, how's it going at catering college? Are you still enjoying it?

SASHA Oh, yes. Well, I haven't been able to go as much lately. With all this happening. I missed a few days. In fact I'm wondering – I'm still considering, actually, whether to leave early. Not finish the course.

CHARMAINE Oh. Why's that?

SASHA I mean, when I first came down here, it seemed like the only thing I really wanted to do. You know, get my certificates. Get some experience. Then later on perhaps, raise a bit of capital, open my own restaurant. That was the limit of my ambitions really. But lately I've been thinking, is that what I really want to do with my life? Possibly end up like my parents. Running a café in some place no one's ever heard of.

During the next, VAL returns with the wine bottle. He watches SASHA from the doorway, as she holds court.

I don't know any more. I'm just not sure. Since I've been down here, in London, so many other possibilities have opened up. For me. Thanks to meeting Val. And I think, do I really want to be stuck in a kitchen all my life? Cooking for other people? Is that the extent of it? I mean, I could run a night club, couldn't I? Travel the world. Become a designer, like you. Be a singer. A television chef. Who knows? I feel right now I could do anything I wanted. Just about anything. No one can stop me. I've got so much in me to give, you see. Val says that all I need is confidence in myself. Go for what you want. Fight for it, if needs be. Don't let anyone get in your way. You step aside for others, you'll never get through the doorway of opportunity yourself, will you? That's what I believe, as well. *(Becoming aware of VAL)* Excuse me. I'll just warm up the soup. Back in a minute.

SASHA *goes off to the kitchen leaving* CHARMAINE *and* ASHLEY *somewhat lost for words.*

VAL Isn't she magic?

As he stares after her affectionately, the lights fade to:

Blackout.

End of Scene Two

Scene Three

A few hours later.

Although the meal is long since over, they are still seated at the table amidst the debris. VAL, ASHLEY *and* CHARMAINE *are well away, laughing and reminiscing.* SASHA, *more subdued now, is clearing a few cheese plates and unwanted glasses. She is feeling slightly sidelined and out of sorts.*

VAL *(in full spate)* ...no, I'll tell you, I'll tell you the best story I ever heard about Morrie. This is absolutely true, this one... He opens this club – out East – Hackney way – well, I say a club – it was a knocking shop with a lock on the door –

ASHLEY Was this the Black Eagle –?

VAL – that's the one – the Black Eagle – *(To* CHARMAINE*)* – you should have seen this club, it was diabolical, Charmaine – and you know the reason he called it that? Because the building used to be – formerly – a branch of Barclays and, when they moved, they left the sign and Morrie – saving money as usual – he had it painted over – and one night – *(To* SASHA*)* – hey, darling, make us all a drop more coffee will you, there's a love –

SASHA *scowls but no one seems to notice her. She goes off to the kitchen.*

– and one night – one night – your lads – our lads – planned to raid the place. Because there's been complaints from all over the neighbourhood, you know – and one lot come in the front – batters down the door – and the other lot come through the back – and they find this big table, all the blokes sitting round it – and these two naked birds on the table with this lighted three-pronged candelabra for some reason – I never worked out the candelabra, but anyway – suddenly the room's full of uniform and Morrie gets up and he says, excuse us officers, if you don't mind, we are in the middle of a fire drill here. Fire drill! *(He laughs)*

They all laugh. SASHA *returns.*

ASHLEY *(laughing)* Fire drill!

CHARMAINE *(screaming with laughter)* Fire drill!

VAL Oh, dear. That's Morrie.

ASHLEY That's Morrie. Dead now.

CHARMAINE Yes, dead now. How did he die, I forget?

VAL Someone shot him.

ASHLEY Shot gun through the chest. Point blank range. Professional. We were scraping him off the walls for weeks.

VAL Yes. One club too many. Foolish boy.

SASHA I put the kettle on.

VAL Good girl.

CHARMAINE I think I once did that candelabra thing, you know. Me and this other girl.

ASHLEY Really, how did it go, then?

VAL Ask her nicely, she'll show you later.

CHARMAINE Oh no, dear, not any more. You have to be supple to do that. *(indicating* SASHA*)* She could do it, probably. I can teach her to do it, if you like, Val.

SASHA Can I get anyone anything else?

VAL You alright, my darling, we're neglecting you, aren't we?

CHARMAINE All these old folk reminiscing.

VAL Very nice meal. Well done.

SASHA Was it?

VAL Of course.

SASHA Only nobody seemed to eat very much.

CHARMAINE We did. I'm full up to bursting.

SASHA You hardly ate anything at all.

CHARMAINE Well, as I said, I'm not that fond of avocado. It tends to quarrel with me.

SASHA You didn't eat the fish, either. Does that quarrel with you as well?

CHARMAINE Well, I have to say dear, if you want me to be perfectly honest, I did find it a wee bit salty for my taste. I mean, as I say, it's only my personal preference but...

SASHA I see. Did everyone else find it too salty? Why didn't they say something?

VAL It wasn't that salty. It was just well seasoned.

ASHLEY I ate the fish. I couldn't eat the vegetables but I ate all the fish.

SASHA Well, I'm sorry. I did my best, I'm sorry. You'd better all eat out next time, hadn't you?

VAL Now, now, now, now... Got her frowning now.

CHARMAINE It was very ambitious dear, you're only just starting out, aren't you? You're only a beginner.

SASHA *appears to be on the verge of tears.*

VAL *(rising)* Sash – *(To the others)* Excuse us, talk among yourselves, will you? – Sash – come over here a minute, come on...

VAL *leads* SASHA *to the sofa and sits down next to her.* CHARMAINE *rises from the table.*

CHARMAINE *(softly, to* ASHLEY*)* I'm just going to the little girls' room.

ASHLEY Right.

VAL *(softly)* Sash...

CHARMAINE *(swaying and stumbling)* Whoops! Who's had a bit too much, then?

CHARMAINE *goes off to the bedrooms.*

VAL *(softly)* Sash. Now, you mustn't get upset like this, darling. You did really well. Your first meal, you did brilliant.

SASHA *(sulkily)* Except nobody liked it and nobody ate it.

VAL Come on. We all liked it. Some of it. Some of it wasn't – well – quite so successful. You were all on your own out there weren't you, that's why. I mean we offered to help, Charmaine offered to help you, didn't she? When you burnt the sauce, she did offer to help.

SASHA I didn't want her in there. I didn't want her in my kitchen with me.

VAL Well, next time, I'll get someone in to help you. How about that? Just to do the ordinary things so you can get on with the creative. Alright?

SASHA I'm never doing this again. Ever.

VAL Well, we'll see, won't we? Tell you what, why don't you entertain us? Just to round things off? Just to round the evening off?

SASHA How do you mean?

VAL Why don't you give us all a song, how about that?

SASHA I can't do that.

VAL Yes you can. I've heard you singing. You've got a beautiful voice.

SASHA I only did it once. In the night club when no one could hear me. I was drunk anyway. I told you, I don't sing in public.

VAL This isn't public, is it? This is just us. You can sing for us, can't you?

SASHA No, I can't!

VAL Sash, I'm asking you, this once. I don't often ask you to do things for me, do I darling? I want to hear you sing. I want them to hear you sing. Come on. It'll make you feel better.

SASHA Don't know what to sing.

VAL You'll think of something, I know you will. Good girl. Thank you.

VAL gets up and leaves SASHA on the sofa. As he does so, CHARMAINE returns. She is still walking unsteadily. Once on her feet, she is now very drunk indeed. Her thin veneer of genteel respectability has entirely gone.

Sash says she's going to sing for us. Just to round off the evening.

CHARMAINE Oh, lovely. That's nice. Make up for the dinner.

ASHLEY Wonderful.

CHARMAINE Is she going to dance as well? Just a minute, I'll fetch a candelabra.

VAL *(cautioning)* Charmaine!

CHARMAINE What are you going to sing for us then, dear?

Silence.

Eh?

VAL *(gently)* Sasha... Come on.

SASHA *(still seated, at length singing)*
NOBODY'S HEART...

VAL *(gently)* Come on now, Sash. Stand up. Do it properly, girl.

SASHA stands and softly starts to sing to them. She is really quite good. She sings very simply with her arms like a schoolgirl's, clasped awkwardly behind her back. Both men are captivated. CHARMAINE looks on, a little more jaundiced.

SASHA *(singing)*
> NOBODY'S HEART BELONGS TO ME,
> HEIGH-HO! WHO CARES?
> NOBODY WRITES HIS SONG TO ME,
> NO ONE BELONGS TO ME,
> THAT'S THE LEAST OF MY CARES.
>
> I MAY BE SAD AT TIMES AND DISINCLINED TO PLAY,
> BUT IT'S NOT BAD AT TIMES,
> TO GO YOUR OWN SWEET WAY.
>
> NOBODY'S ARMS BELONG TO ME,
> NO ARMS FEEL STRONG TO ME,
> I ADMIRE THE MOON
> AS A MOON,
> JUST A MOON,
> NOBODY'S HEART BELONGS TO ME TODAY. *

*Rodgers & Hart, 1942.

SASHA *finishes.* **ASHLEY** *is deeply moved. He sniffs and blows his nose.*

ASHLEY *(tearfully, at length)* That just about sums it all up, really, doesn't it? Life?

VAL *(sadly, also quite moved)* Beautiful, Sash, beautiful, girl.

SASHA Thank you. *(She sits again).*

Silence for a moment.

CHARMAINE Well, bloody hell, darling, that's a real downer, isn't it? You want to take a tip from me, dear, you want to get the fellers going don't sing them miserable bloody songs like that...

SASHA Sorry?

VAL Now, now...

CHARMAINE I mean, look at 'em now, it's like a sodding funeral parlour. You want to get 'em going, splashing out with the readies, you've got to try a bit harder than that, love. *(Rising)*

Here look, sex! Put a bit of sex in it! That's what they want, dear, that's all they come for, bit of sex. Misery? They can get that at home, darling. They come to a club, they want sex. A good time. That's what you're selling them. So you need to sell it. You get up and sing that in a club they'll be stampeding out the doors!

VAL *(dangerously)* Charmaine, that's enough! Leave it alone!

CHARMAINE No, I'm telling her, Val, I'm telling the girl. The kid needs to know, doesn't she? If she wants to go singing in clubs. She's got a sweet little voice and nice little body, but she's not going to get nowhere, is she, if she stands up there and sings like some fucking choirboy – Use your body, love. That's what it's there for... *(Demonstrating, singing)* MY HEART BELONGS TO DADDY! DEE-DEE-DEE! DEE-DEE-DAA! DEE-DEE-DEE!

SASHA *(screaming suddenly)* Stop it!

VAL *(violently, simultaneously)* I said that's enough, Charmaine!

CHARMAINE *(startled)* What?

VAL Now get your stuff, you're out of here! I said out! NOW!

Silence. **CHARMAINE** *is suddenly sober and quite frightened. So is* **SASHA**. *This is a side to* **VAL** *she has never before encountered.*

CHARMAINE *(in a tiny voice)* All I was doing, Val, was...

VAL *(softly)* Hey! Don't ever argue with me. *(Stabbing at her face with his finger)* Never. Ever. Argue. With. Me. Again. Right?

CHARMAINE *(in a whisper)* Right.

VAL Get your coat and go home.

CHARMAINE Yes, I'll – *(She looks round vaguely)*

SASHA *(making as if to rise)* It's in the bedroom, I'll –

VAL No, let her get it, Sash. She can get it herself. She knows where the bedroom is.

CHARMAINE *goes off meekly.*

ASHLEY I think you're in danger of over-reacting a bit here, Val. I mean, she was only –

VAL You keep out of this, alright?

ASHLEY *(to* **SASHA***)* I don't know what she was on about. I thought what you did was very sexy. Very sexy indeed.

VAL *glares at him.* **SASHA** *smiles faintly.* **CHARMAINE** *returns with her coat. She holds her mobile.*

CHARMAINE Would it be alright if I phoned for a taxi, Val?

VAL No, you phone for one in the street. Go on. You've outstayed your welcome in here.

CHARMAINE *puts her mobile away and obediently moves to the door.*

(calling her back) Hey!

CHARMAINE Yes?

VAL Don't you think you owe your hostess an apology, then?

CHARMAINE *looks at* **SASHA.**

Then apologise to her. Go on.

SASHA It's alright, I –

VAL Go on!

CHARMAINE I'm sorry, Sasha. I didn't mean to upset you.

VAL That's better. Now get off home, you stupid drunken bitch!

CHARMAINE *opens the front door and leaves.*

ASHLEY *(rising)* Oh, come on, Val. It's two in the bloody morning, you can't leave the woman wandering the streets at this time of night, can you?

ASHLEY *goes off after* CHARMAINE.

VAL *(after him)* Why not? You don't want to worry about her, she's used to it. Spent the best years of her life doing that, didn't she?

VAL *is aware of* SASHA *staring at him. He pauses, attempting to regain some composure.*

Sometimes you need to... You have to be firm. With people like that. Know what I mean? They get out of hand. They take advantage. You give them something. Out of the goodness of your heart. You're generous with them, they take advantage of you. They take it for granted. They revert...if you like...to their true nature. Know what I mean? Animals. It makes me mad when people take advantage of my good nature, that's all. Know what I mean? I mean, her behaviour just then...to you...you...unforgivable. Wasn't it? *(Pause)* Know what I mean?

SASHA *(dead)* I'll clear the rest of this. Put them in the dishwasher.

The flat doorbell rings. SASHA *opens the door.* ASHLEY *enters again.*

ASHLEY God takes care of drunks, eh? There was a cab just dropping someone off next door.

SASHA *takes some dirty plates and glasses from the table through to the kitchen.*

You had no business talking to her like that. Talk about over-reaction.

VAL Mind your own business.

ASHLEY It became my business. I was here. I saw it. You can't talk to people like that, Val, not any more. You may have done that in the old days, pal, when you meant something, but you're just a sad old git now and you ought to know better.

VAL Speak for yourself.

ASHLEY A sad old git with more money than he knows what to do with, playing around with young girls, treating them like Barbie dolls.

VAL You keep out of this.

ASHLEY What? She lets you dress her up in the morning, does she? Choose her dress out the wardrobe for her?

VAL Oh, go home, you sad old bastard.

ASHLEY You're destroying that girl. Little by little you're destroying her.

VAL Jealous or what?

ASHLEY I mean it, Val. You've only got to look at her! Like a bloody call girl.

VAL Listen, are you going or do I have to...?

ASHLEY Have to what? What? What are you going to do, eh?

VAL Throw you out, if needs be.

ASHLEY Oh, yes? Going to call for nephew Frankie, are you?

VAL No need for that.

ASHLEY He's so fat these days he can barely get into the car any more. Maybe she'll do it for you. Sasha. She's in better shape than you are, I tell you.

VAL You little bastard...

ASHLEY Come on! Come on then, Val! Let's see what you can do, boy!

VAL Alright...

> **VAL** *lunges at* **ASHLEY** *and the two men struggle. Initially,* **VAL** *appears to be getting the better of it.*

VAL *(triumphantly, as they struggle)* Told you not to try it, Ashley, didn't I? Now who's an old git, eh? Who's an old git? Say it!

ASHLEY *suddenly has trouble breathing. He starts to wheeze. He is in some pain. He releases* VAL *and grabs a piece of furniture for support and then drops to his knees and doubles over, his head touching the carpet.*

(in pain) Oh, God!

VAL *(standing back, triumphantly)* Look at you! Pathetic old git! Try this!

He shapes to take a vicious kick at the prostrate ASHLEY *and promptly pulls up in agony.*

(crying out) Oh, God! My knee! My knee! My knee's gone!

VAL *hops in agony on his good-ish leg. Ashley pulls himself up on his knees again, gasping for air. At this point, Sasha returns from the kitchen. She looks on in amazement.*

SASHA What are you both doing?

ASHLEY Sasha, could you...?

VAL Sasha, never mind him, help me please. It's locked!

ASHLEY Help me!

VAL My knee! Just help me into the chair, Sasha...

ASHLEY Sasha, please!

SASHA *looks from one to the other, uncertain who to help.*

The desk phone rings. They all stop. SASHA *goes and answers it.*

SASHA Hallo? ...Yes... Yes, it is... Yes... Oh, no... Is she –?

...But is she –? ...Right, I will. Straight away. *(She rings off)* That was the hospital. It's Chloë. I have to go.

SASHA *rushes off to the bedroom.*

ASHLEY Where's she going?

VAL Where are you going, Sash?

SASHA *returns with her coat.*

SASHA Chloë's been in an accident. I have to go!

VAL Accident?

ASHLEY Where?

SASHA She fell in front of a train. On the Northern Line. *(She opens the front door)* She says someone tried to push her.

SASHA *goes out, closing the door.*

The two men look at each other. As they do so, the lights fade to:

Blackout.

End of Scene Three

Scene Four

The same. The next morning.

SASHA *still tidying from the night before.*

She is moving about quietly, as if not to disturb someone. She is dressed casually, more like her old self.

There is a soft knocking on the flat's front door. So quiet that **SASHA** *barely hears it.*

She pauses in her task. The knock is repeated. **SASHA** *goes and opens the door.*

It is **ASHLEY.**

SASHA *(muted)* Hallo.

ASHLEY Sorry, I wasn't sure if you might still be asleep. I heard you creeping in very late.

SASHA Come in.

ASHLEY steps inside. **SASHA** *closes the door. There is something quite distant in her manner.*

We didn't get back till after three. Chloë's still asleep.

ASHLEY Well, I won't stay long. Just wanted to make sure... you know.

SASHA Thank you. I think we'd have a job to wake her. She'd already been sedated and when she got in she took a sleeping pill on top of that. And her room's pretty soundproof these days. With the new wallpaper.

ASHLEY With the white fur?

SASHA Blocks out all the sound. Great for London. She'd had trouble sleeping before, you see.

ASHLEY Is she...alright?

SASHA I think so. I think it was an accident. I don't think anyone actually tried to push her. She slipped on the platform. In some ice cream. Someone managed to catch her. I think it was just an accident. *(Reflecting)* At least I hope it was. *(Clearing away some more)* You sort out your differences last night then, you two?

ASHLEY We – came to an arrangement.

SASHA Glad to hear it.

ASHLEY That we'd try and find different planets to live on.

SASHA Sensible.

> **ASHLEY** *watches her.*

ASHLEY Sasha...

SASHA He'll be round here in a minute, if you don't want to run into him.

ASHLEY Listen...

SASHA I just phoned him. Asked him to come.

ASHLEY Look, you do need to know a few things.

SASHA *(going out)* He's on his way.

ASHLEY About him. There's things you need to know.

> **SASHA** *goes into the kitchen.*

SASHA *(offstage)* No, I don't. I told you. Not from you.

ASHLEY There's things I didn't say about him, that I should have said, that I never said. Because if I did say them, I thought you might have thought I was saying them for – inappropriate personal reasons. So I didn't say them. But after last night...

> **SASHA** *returns from the kitchen.*

SASHA There's not much you can tell me about him, Ashley. I promise you.

ASHLEY Oh, there is. Believe me there is. Last night I saw you with those two, him and Charmaine, you singing that song, like – like you did – and I thought – she looks so – vulnerable... so <u>fragile</u>. Don't take that the wrong way...

SASHA *(stopping, smiling)* Sit down a minute, Ashley, will you? Go on, sit down.

ASHLEY *does so.* SASHA *sits, facing him.*

You don't know an awful lot about women, do you?

ASHLEY Well, I think, I've had my – you know – I've had – my share –

SASHA No, I'm not talking about having them. I'm talking about understanding them. Plenty of blokes sleep with them. Very few actually understand them. Still, why should they bother, eh? If they can get away without, why bother? You can't blame them altogether. We're not much better. I sometimes think there's a lot of women who don't properly understand either.

ASHLEY Women who don't understand men, you mean?

SASHA No, women who don't understand women. Everybody understands men, there's never a problem with them. But look at Charmaine last night. Wiggling her arse and laying down the law to me about sex. What she knows about sex you could write on a G string.

ASHLEY She's certainly not as sexy as you. Not in a million years.

SASHA Oh, I know that.

She smiles. ASHLEY *smiles back at her.*

ASHLEY I wish I'd had a daughter like you.

SASHA I think that might have been a bit dangerous, mightn't it? Did you never have any children at all, you and your wife?

ASHLEY Yes, we had one daughter. But she – since Monica and I split up – she – Jenny won't have much to do with me, I'm afraid...

SASHA Ah. Sad. Well, they go through that phase sometimes, kids. Don't they? But they usually grow out of it in time.

ASHLEY Bit late now, she's forty-seven.

SASHA Yes, of course, she would be. All I'm saying is, don't worry about me, Ashley. Really. There's whole areas of life – most areas in life, if I'm perfectly honest, that I know nothing about. I'm still learning about. But there's other areas – you'd be surprised.

The downstairs buzzer sounds.

There he is.

ASHLEY *(going to the door and opening it)* Give me a moment to get downstairs. I don't want to run into him. I might deck him. See you – around. I hope.

ASHLEY *goes off.*

SASHA Maybe. Bye.

The door buzzer sounds again.

SASHA *waits with the door open till she hears the door of* **ASHLEY**'s *flat close. She picks up the entryphone.*

(into the phone) Hallo, come up.

She buzzes the front door and replaces the phone. She leaves the flat door ajar. She moves back into the room and prepares herself.

VAL *enters and closes the door.*

VAL Cold out there today.

SASHA It looks it. I haven't been out yet this morning, I...

VAL You got her home safe, then?

SASHA Yes. She's still asleep.

VAL She really thinks someone tried to push her?

SASHA Yes.

VAL What, under a train?

SASHA That's what she said.

VAL Who'd want to do that?

SASHA No idea. The same blokes who shoved a cell phone up her boyfriend's arse, perhaps. Who knows? *(She stares at him)*

VAL What happened to her was nothing to do with me, Sash. I promise you.

SASHA I never said it was.

VAL Well. I'd hate you to think it was.

SASHA They believe now it was probably an accident.

VAL Ah. Well. Thank God, eh?

SASHA It's a little bit alarming, though, you felt the need to deny it at all, isn't it?

Pause. **VAL** *stares at her.*

(rather sadly) We have to stop this, don't we?

VAL If this is about last night –

SASHA No, it's not really about that –

VAL – I'll be the first to admit I'd had a few too many. But then we were all a bit out of order –

SASHA – I'm saying, it's not about last night. That was – just a – symptom, wasn't it? A sign of things to come. Wasn't it?

VAL How do you mean?

SASHA We've sort of – exhausted each other really Val, haven't we? Me trying to be someone I wasn't, to please you... Always pretending. And you –

VAL What do you mean, pretending?

SASHA Just like you're pretending to me, Val. Always have been.

VAL Listen, if you're unhappy, in any way, you just have to –

SASHA What do you mean, unhappy? I loved it. Every second.
Never been happier. What woman wouldn't have loved all
this? Being treated like a princess? People at her beck and
call. Never having to worry about money. Magic! But all the
same, it was pretending, wasn't it? Couldn't last for ever.
For either of us, could it, Val? Honestly? Look, I saw a side
of you last night I never want to see again.

VAL Listen, that was me looking out for you, that's all that was.

SASHA I did know that part of you existed – it had to – well,
maybe not from day one I didn't but from day three, say,
I knew it was probably there. Somewhere. Had to be. But
because you chose to hide it from me, I chose to ignore it.
But I knew it was there, Val. I know you've done some really
terrible things in your life, I know you have –

VAL How can you know that? Who've you been talking to, eh?
Ashley? Listen, did I ever treat you badly?

SASHA No! But I see it in other people, Val. In their faces. All
those women. Yes, they all make out they love you because
you've seen them right but underneath they're still all
terrified to death of you.

VAL Bollocks.

SASHA Like Charmaine last night. One look from you, she
nearly wet herself.

VAL She deserved that.

SASHA Nobody deserves that. Nobody.

VAL Anyway. I'd never do that to you. You know that.

Pause.

So. What do I have to do to make you happy, then? Get my
little girl smiling again, eh?

SASHA *(sadly)* You have to let her go, Val.

VAL What if I won't?

SASHA Then you'd be treating her like you treated Charmaine. Only worse.

VAL *paces about. He is getting angry.*

VAL Oh, this is bollocks. It's all bollocks! Come on! Look, maybe I pretended with you. Maybe I – embroidered my past life a little –

SASHA A little –?

VAL Alright – a lot! Everyone does that a bit, don't they? But you had complete freedom, Sash, you were always free, weren't you? Free to come and go. You had everything you wanted, didn't you? Every single thing you asked for? And I never asked for nothing in return. Except your company. What more do you bloody want?

SASHA To be me! I want to be me again!

VAL What you talking about? You are you. Who the hell else are you? You are you!

SASHA I'm not. I'm really not. I don't know who I am. I'm what I think you want me to be.

VAL Listen, I know you better than you know yourself, girl. I've been round the block a few times, I can tell you.

SASHA Well, I'll tell you this, Val. You don't know me. Not at all you don't! You know – *(Indicating)* – that much of me because that's the bit I chose to show you. Right? But there's other bits, I tell you, you wouldn't want to know at all. Not at all. This little princess, she can be a right pain in the arse, I can tell you. She's got a foul temper, she sulks and screams till she gets her own way, she's deliberately cruel sometimes, she uses people, she's selfish and greedy and secretly she eats like a pig – and as a result she's got a bum that's permanently covered in spots. That enough to be going on with, is it?

A silence. VAL *considers this.*

VAL I hate it when women run themselves down.

SASHA *(frustratedly)* Oh, dear God! *(She sinks her head in her hands)*

VAL You've changed, you know. Since we first met. You've changed.

SASHA No, I haven't. Ask my parents, they'll vouch for me, I promise you. I was always spoilt and horrible.

VAL I've changed you. Ashley was right. My hands are covered in – dirt. So that everything I touch, I finish up making dirty. You can't change yourself, Sash, you're absolutely right. Much as I pretended to you, in the end you can never run away from it, can you? Yourself?

SASHA *(softly)* That's what I'm saying.

VAL I saw you only a few months ago and I saw something so pure, so radiant...

SASHA *(murmuring)* Fragile...

VAL Fragile, yes, that as well. And I should never have touched you, girl. You were never for me. I should have left you where you were. I was like a bloody stone age man picking up – I don't know – a Michelangelo. You're right.

SASHA That's not what I meant.

VAL I thought with you, girl, I maybe could make it right. Next time I'll stick to bloody Barbie dolls, eh?

SASHA What?

VAL Assuming I have a next time.

SASHA Val, what are you talking about, now?

VAL Listen. I don't know how we sort this out. Everything. I mean, as far as I'm concerned, anything I gave you was a gift and you can keep it. If you feel you don't want it, that it's tainted in some way –

SASHA *(irritated)* Oh, for God's sake!

VAL No, I'll understand. I really will.

Silence.

Right. I'll be off then.

SASHA Just like that?

VAL I don't hang around, girl. Not at my age. I got to be at this charity lunch, anyway. Listen, I'll still be looking out for you. Any problems, anyone gives you trouble, landlords, whatever, you ring your Uncle Val, alright? On your new mobile. Whatever else you give away, you hang on to that, eh?

SASHA *(smiling but suddenly a little tearful as well)* Yes.

VAL You can send me pictures of yourself, if you want.

SASHA I will.

VAL You know, clean ones. You know. Nothing like that.

SASHA No, nothing like that. *(Suddenly weeping)* Oh, God, it's been such fun!

VAL *(quite moved himself)* Hasn't it just?

SASHA We've had so many laughs...

VAL Yes, we've had a few of them, haven't we? *(Producing a handkerchief)* Here, princess, you dry your eyes now. Don't want to end like this, do we? We never have tears, do we? No frowns. Not between us. Not allowed.

SASHA I know. I'm sorry. Not allowed.

She pulls herself together.

(rather formally) Thank you for everything, Uncle Val. I probably will return a lot of things to you because you've given me so much. But if I could keep the mobile phone and the dishwasher for starters, that would be great.

VAL Anything you want, girl.

SASHA *(hugging him tightly)* Thank you.

VAL No. Thank you.

He prises her gently away from him and opens the door.

Bye bye Sash. Take care.

SASHA Bye.

VAL And keep away from that bastard downstairs, he's a very bad influence.

VAL *goes out, closing the door.*

Alone, SASHA *gives a little wail to herself.* CHLOË *comes on from the bedroom. She is limping slightly from her accident.*

CHLOË I woke up just now, I thought I'd fallen asleep inside a polar bear's arse. Who were you talking to?

SASHA The window cleaner. I was just paying him off.

CHLOË Really? *(Looking at the windows)* He didn't do a very good job, did he?

SASHA No.

CHLOË Presumably that's why you're crying.

Slight pause.

(sitting) You know, I slept surprisingly well. Maybe that bed's alright. The sheets are so loud they sing you to sleep. Is there any tea?

Pause.

I'll make some in a minute, then.

Pause.

Who was that just now? Val?

SASHA *(muted)* Yes. He just – came to say good-bye. We decided it was time to stop. He was – getting to be a bad influence.

CHLOË Oh. Does that mean you've got to give everything back?

SASHA Some of it.

CHLOË We can keep the table, I hope? That works rather well just there. And the sofa?

SASHA I thought you hated everything?

CHLOË Some of it. I loathe the pictures. I could maybe live with some of it.

SASHA You're staying then?

CHLOË Do you mind? I just don't think I can stand another bijou hotel.

SASHA I'm sorry I shouted.

CHLOË We both shouted, didn't we? We're sisters. That's what sisters do.

SASHA Half sisters.

CHLOË Well, half the time they do, anyway.

Slight pause.

Do you know, I phoned Zack from the hospital, to tell him what had happened. To me. He'd gone home to his mother. She answered his mobile. His bloody mobile! Can you believe that? She said he was too upset to speak to me. When I think, when he was in hospital, I rushed to his side, didn't I –?

SASHA Forget him. You really must.

CHLOË Yes.

SASHA *(scowling)* You're never to mention his name again, do you hear? Every time you do, you know, you frown.

CHLOË I do?

SASHA It's bad for your complexion, for one thing. What's more, it makes me very angry, too. I'll make the tea.

CHLOË Oh my God! No. Let me. I'll do it! Anything to keep you happy.

CHLOË *goes off to the kitchen.* SASHA *studies herself in the mirror.*

SASHA *(to herself)* God! Do with an early night myself.

CHLOË'*s mobile phone rings.*

(calling) CHLOË –

She checks herself and studies the display. After a second she answers it.

(into phone) Hallo...no, Zack, it's me, Sasha... No, she's – busy at the moment... She's too upset to talk to you...yes... Listen, Zack, I'm glad you called, I wanted a word with you. Listen, I think you should stop seeing Chloë, I really do, I don't think you're good for her...no, I don't frankly...well, she's my sister for one thing...no, listen... Zack...listen to me... I'm only going to say this once... Are you listening? Now, I'm sorry to hear about your unfortunate episode with those two gentlemen... I'm glad you got your phone back safe...but I promise if you don't leave my sister alone, Zack, I'll arrange for them to meet you again and this time it won't just be your mobile, next time it'll be your whole fucking laptop, you hear me? *(Savagely)* Now piss off, you pillock!

She disconnects and tosses the phone back on to the chair. She smiles to herself. CHLOË *re-enters from the kitchen.*

CHLOË Was that my phone?

SASHA No.

CHLOË Oh. Only I thought it might be... *(Catching* SASHA'*s expression)* Sorry. Forget him. Yes. Smile. *(She smiles)* New life, yes?

SASHA *smiles and holds out her hand to her sister.*

SASHA Yes. For both of us.

CHLOË *takes her hand. A moment, as they stand and smile at each other.*

(briskly) Now where the hell's that tea? Come on, girl! Tea! Tea! Tea! Tea!

She pushes CHLOË *in front of her and slaps her affectionately on the rump and drives her sister squealing indignantly into the kitchen.*

CHLOË *exits.* SASHA *remains briefly. She surveys the room.*

(to herself) New Life!

As she leaves, a blackout.

End of Play

PROPS

ACT ONE
Clothes and belongings (p1)
One or two Christmas cards (p1)
A tiny, battered, artificial tree (p1)
Sofa (p1)
Armchair (p1)
Coffee table (p1)
Extendable dining table and three chairs (p1)
Desk strewn with papers (p1)
Phone (p1)
Laptop (p1)
Sideboard with drawers & cupboards (p1)
Entry phone (p1)
Sachet of tablets (p3)
Glass of water (p3)
Mobile (p8)
Huge bunch of expensive looking flowers (p21)
Card (p21)
Room is comparatively tidier (p23)
Chloë is laying the table (p23)
Romantic candle lit dinner for two (p23)
Mobile (p23)
Bags (p23)
Smart dress shop carrier bag (p23)
Bottle of water (p23)
Opened bottle of claret (p24)
Small bunch of flowers (p26)
Empty wine bottle (p32)
Half empty bottle of gin (p32)
Glass (p32)
Papers (p36)
Glass of water (p36)
Chloë's mobile (p37)
Both carrying carrier bags apparently from smart clothing and
shoe shops (p44)

ACT TWO

'Proper furniture' – new carpet, sofa, armchair, coffee table, dining table, chairs, sideboard and replacement high-tech desk for Chloë (p53)
Packages (p58)
Duty free bags (p58)
Suitcases etc. (p58)
Gift wrapped package (p62)
New table is laid rather elaborately for dinner for four (p64)
Fresh candles (p64)
New candle holder (p64)
Two glasses of white wine (p66)
Two glasses (p69)
Glass of wine (p73)
Plate of home-made canapés (p77)
Wine bottle (p78)
Still seated at the table amidst the debris (p79)
Cheese plates and unwanted glasses (p79)
Mobile (p86)
Dirty plates and glasses (p87)
Handkerchief (p99)

LIGHTING

ACT ONE

Outside it is dark, at the start the room is lit only from the street lights outside (p1)
Light from the landing illuminates the room (p2)
Sasha switches on the lights (p2)
Blackout (p22)
Blackout (p31)
The room is only dimly lit by the street lights through the curtains (p32)
Switches on the lights (p32)
Sasha enters, the hall light behind her (p32)
Blackout (p43)
Room is in darkness except for street lighting from the windows (p44)
Sasha switches on the room lights (p52)

Val switches off the light (p52)
Blackout (p52)

ACT TWO
Lights fade to: blackout (p63)
Lights fade to: blackout (p78
Lights fade to: blackout (p90)
Blackout (p103)

SOUND EFFECTS

ACT ONE
Can hear the continuous rumble of city traffic (p1)
Sound of a key in the lock (p2)
Sound of a key in the front door (p13)
Chloë's mobile rings (p15)
Chloë's mobile rings again (p19)
Front door buzzer rings (p20)
Front door buzzer rings (p25)
Flat doorbell rings (p25)
Mobile beeps (p29)
Mobile beeps again (p30)
Sound of a key softly in the front door lock (p31)
Key in the front door and the sound of Sasha and Val laughing (p43)
Flat doorbell rings (p46)

ACT TWO
From the kitchen, an effortful grunt (p52)
Another grunt from the kitchen (p52)
A key in the flat's front door (p57)
Offstage, Chloë screams (p59)
Another scream offstage (p59)
We hear it (package) shatter against the wall (p62)
The new high-fi is softly playing classical music (p63)
From the kitchen, a timer starts beeping (p66)

The beeping stops (p67)
The flat doorbell rings (p67)
Front door buzzer sounds (p71)
Flat doorbell rings (p86)
Desk phone rings (p88)
Sort knocking at the flat's front door (p90)
Knock is repeated (p90)
Downstairs buzzer sounds (p93)
Door buzzer sounds again (p93)
She buzzes the front door (p93)
Chloë's mobile phone rings (p101)

VISIT THE SAMUEL FRENCH BOOKSHOP AT THE ROYAL COURT THEATRE

Browse plays and theatre books, get expert advice and enjoy a coffee

Samuel French Bookshop
Royal Court Theatre
Sloane Square
London
SW1W 8AS
020 7565 5024

Shop from thousands of titles on our website

 samuelfrench.co.uk

 samuelfrenchltd

 samuel french uk

Lightning Source UK Ltd.
Milton Keynes UK
UKHW051917020219
336564UK00012B/654/P

9 780573 116025